UNITED NATIONS

United Nations:

Hope for a Divided World

by SIR LESLIE MUNRO

HENRY HOLT AND COMPANY · · · NEW YORK

FIRST EDITION

Library of Congress Catalog Card Number: 60-5819

The quotation on the last page of this book is from
The Mind and Faith of Justice Holmes by Max
Lerner, Little, Brown & Co., Boston, 1943.

85893-0110

Printed in the United States of America

Contents

Contents

UNITED NATIONS

Foreword

IN MARCH, 1959, AS THE SPECIAL REPRESENTATIVE OF THE
Secretary-General I visited Korea. My mission was to make
an agreement with the Korean government concerning the
United Nations cemetery. When I came to Pusan on a spring
morning the cloudless sky, the wind, the earth breathed life,
but all about me were the white wooden crosses of the dead.
Pusan lies at the tip of Korea, that Asian peninsula which
has been the battleground chosen by both the Tsars and the
Communists for the domination of the Far East. Buried at
Pusan are some 2,000 soldiers who died fighting the Com-
munists from North Korea and China; the bodies of the
American dead have been brought back to the United States.
The cemetery at Pusan is surrounded by green hills on three
sides, and the fourth faces the sparkling sea; here are the
graves of soldiers from fifteen countries: Australia, Belgium,
Canada, Colombia, Ethiopia, France, Greece, Luxembourg,
the Netherlands, New Zealand, the Philippines, Thailand,
Turkey, the Union of South Africa, the United Kingdom.
With the Americans and beside the South Koreans, all these
men from so far away fought and died under the banner of
the United Nations. Their purpose: to throw back and defeat
aggression.

As I laid a wreath on behalf of the United Nations an
honour guard saluted. I was there to do honour, amid a great

silence, to the men who could not speak but whose young voices I seemed to hear whispering, "Surely we have not died in vain." This is the challenge to us all.

I also went to the demilitarized zone in Panmunjom. I came there in the evening and from a lookout post I saw the blue hills of Communist North Korea. A desolate valley stretched before me, and across a stream was the Bridge of No Return: no return for those who after the armistice chose to walk the bridge and go back behind the curtain. Like the cemetery at Pusan the place was silent, not with the quiet for those who would rise again but with a brooding, melancholy silence of a stilled battleground, broken suddenly by the whirring of the wings of pheasants. This was the no man's land between communism and freedom. Korea is still divided; there is an armistice but not peace.

I felt profoundly this division which has split the world as none in history, not even when the barbarians threatened Rome. For it is a division of men's minds, and it strikes at the very basis of a world organization which, though it is called the United Nations, is not united so long as Communist imperialism makes coexistence only an aspiration. Yet in an imperfect and divided world we have to strive to live together. We owe that to the dead and to the living. We owe it to ourselves in the nuclear age if we have the will to survive.

My journey to Korea confirmed my faith in the United Nations, for here the organization was the symbol against aggression. As I stood at Panmunjom and Pusan, so remote from my work in New York and Washington, I thought of man's endless quest for peace, of his readiness to die if thereby his brothers might survive. I saw my fellow human beings in Korea huddled in poverty, yet cheerful and virile. The Koreans I watched swarming in Seoul had for the most part, I suppose, never heard of the men who, as the last war ground to a close, planned the United Nations. But whether they knew this or not, these Koreans, in spite of ordeals and isolation, were to me reminders of the oneness of a shrinking world. I, from faraway New Zealand, knew as I worked in Seoul that Tokio, Manila, Jakarta, Saigon, San Francisco, Hawaii, and Vladivostok were indeed my country's neighbours in the Pacific.

Over a century ago Macaulay spoke of the day, which he obviously thought remote, when some traveller from New Zealand, in the midst of a vast solitude, might take his stand on a broken arch on London Bridge to sketch the ruins of St. Paul's.

Even though he had a quirk for omniscience, Macaulay with all his Victorian certitude would have been surprised at the birth of the United Nations out of a global conflict. His surprise would have been greater if he had found that a New Zealander, from a country which in his day knew few white men, would in 1957 be President of the Assembly of nations of a world organization. Macaulay might have been surprised, although he certainly would have been thankful, to see St. Paul's survive the holocaust. The great dependency of India, whose eventual self-government Macaulay contemplated, is now split into two republics within the British Commonwealth, which with New Zealand are members of the United Nations. India and Pakistan are two of several Asian nations to gain both independence and membership in the international community, where Europe is no longer predominant. Even Macaulay might have been astounded to hear the leader of India speaking in terms of authority to the West and after Tibet, of sorrow and rebuke to India's northern neighbour.

In Africa and Asia, with varying fortunes, men are on the march toward independence and prosperity. The dawn is breaking on a new world, whose inhabitants have suddenly found they can penetrate the universe.

In a spirit of optimism despite our troubled times, I mention these African and Asian developments which find their counterparts in other continents. All the peoples who have gained statehood have become members of the United Nations and have voiced their hopes and their fears in its halls. If they hope too much from it, they still fear to give it much authority where their own sovereign powers are concerned. I do not hesitate to write of the weaknesses of the United Nations; rather they are the weaknesses of its members than of itself.

Let us take courage. In the century and a half following the Napoleonic Wars, mankind has made astonishing national and international progress with endless resiliency, in spite of terrible wars and the division of the world imposed by communism.

Aspirations and endeavours must be great where despair and failures can be so grave. One of the chief forces serving to unite mankind is the United Nations. I say "one" because as a citizen of the Commonwealth and a former Ambassador to the United States, I know the benefits of a world-wide Commonwealth unity. I believe, too, that without the bulwark of Anglo-American co-operation the United Nations is gravely weakened. When that co-operation does not exist, as in the Suez crisis, the United Nations lacks its most cohesive element. Only the Communists should then rejoice.

Fortunately for us, the wounds of Suez to joint Anglo-American policy have been healed; thanks in particular to the patient, skilful determination and distaste for recrimination characteristic of the Prime Minister of Great Britain, Harold Macmillan, who knows that the mainspring of Western policy, whether in the United Nations or outside it, is Anglo-American unity of purpose and planning. In fact when, toward the end of the last Great War, the proposals for a world organization were being considered in the United States, Anglo-American co-operation was taken for granted; a mistake as the events of 1956 proved. We in the Western world can take nothing for granted.

It was the co-operation of the Soviet with the West during the peace, which was in doubt in 1944 and 1945. Mr. Churchill wrote in *Triumph and Tragedy* that he felt "bound to proclaim (his) confidence in Soviet good faith in the hope of procuring it." Those with the benefit of hindsight might ponder a great statesman's approach, which he thought unavoidable, to a doubtful and difficult future.

Today we have a United Nations almost universal in its membership, stronger than the League of Nations through the accession of the United States, and more dynamic and viable because of the provisions of the Charter for economic and social development and for advancement of dependent territories toward self-government or independence.

For over fourteen years the United Nations has been in the forefront of world news, although the sober and constructive aspect of its work in the Economic and Social Council and the Trusteeship Council has not received wide publicity.

While the average intelligent citizen usually has a working knowledge of the constitution of his own state, few, even among politicians, know much about the status, powers, and functions of the United Nations. Casual, even constant, newspaper reading is unlikely to remove this deficiency. Indeed several governments are in the habit of sending politicians, who are not members of a Cabinet or Ministry, as members of delegations to New York so that they may learn the composition and procedures of the Assembly and study and participate in its debates on matters of international significance.

Ignorance of the aims and the authority of the United Nations ranges from those who regard it as a world legislature to those who dismiss it as a futile or dangerous debating society. "Better," as Sir Winston has said, "to jaw than to war."

I have felt impelled to write this book, not for scholars and international lawyers but to acquaint the general public with the objects and the powers of the United Nations and with some of the crises it has handled and survived. I hope that they will be helped by a record of some of my experiences and dealings with the great who have assisted in the debates of the world organization. I shall write of what it is and what it is not.

Many speak of a success or a failure of the United Nations as if it were an entity apart from its members. It is, in the sense that it employs an extensive staff, that it can own or lease land, erect buildings, make treaties and agreements with governments and appoint representatives to them.

But in the political sense the United Nations is only an instrument of its members for them to use or not, as the majority of them may decide. Accordingly when an editorial in terms of lofty disdain says that the United Nations has failed in a given situation, what the newspapers should have said is that the majority of the members of the United Nations, which in all probability include the editor's own government, have failed to realise the expectations of editorial policy. When an editorial says that a new situation will be a test for the United Nations, the learned writer sitting in his ivory tower should have written that the situation will be a test for the wisdom, the courage, or the forbearance of all the governments which are members of the United Nations.

The classic cases are the Suez and Hungarian crises. I suppose that in the United States many, if not most people, would say that the United Nations succeeded in the Suez crisis and failed over Hungary.

Let us analyse this conclusion. In 1956 the overwhelming majority of the members of the Assembly, led by the United States, stopped the British, the French, and the Israelis at Suez. The governments of these three nations bowed before this manifestation of world public opinion: they withdrew their troops and left the Egyptian government in complete control of the Suez Canal.

We are too close to events to assess all the consequences of the United Nations' intervention in the Suez affair, in particular to conclude whether its handling of the crisis was a link in the chain of events leading to the present troubled situation in Iraq. But I think we can say that the steps approved by the overwhelming majority of the members of the Assembly in 1956 resulted in one outstanding success: the swift establishment of the United Nations Emergency Force.

But, say the critics of the United Nations, the organization failed over Hungary. What do they mean by this? Do they suggest that the United Nations, as an instrument to be viewed apart from its members, failed to rescue the Hungarians from the Russians? Are they suggesting, as some do, that the Secretary-General at the very earliest stage of Russian intervention should have gone to Hungary?

Consider the last question. In recent years the Secretary-General has taken the initiative conferred on him by the Charter but usually, if not invariably, after consultation with the Great Powers and the other countries particularly involved. It is hard to see, given the Kremlin's determination to keep Hungary irrevocably behind the Iron Curtain, what good could have come from a visit by Mr. Hammarskjold to Budapest, even if the Communists had permitted him to enter Hungary while battle raged.

We come to the major point: that the Assembly itself failed over Hungary. But the Assembly acts on the votes of its members. Even a majority of votes would have little practical effect on a grave occasion unless the majority of the Great Powers concurred. In other words, if the more powerful members are unwilling to act, the United Nations can do nothing very effective. There is no evidence that the United States, in all the course of the lengthy Assembly debates over Hungary, was ever ready to invoke sanctions against the Soviet: sanctions which in all probability would have led to war, a nuclear world war.

Some may say that the Suez crisis, coinciding with the Hungarian, prevented the United Nations from acting to save Hungary. I am ready to concede that this coincidence of the Suez crisis was a help to the Soviet. It may be that if there had been no Suez crisis, the United States and Britain together would have moved the United Nations to intervene in Hungary. Merely to put the hypothesis, however, is to emphasise the gravity of the issue. I solemnly doubt whether at any stage Washington and London were ready to risk a Third World War to secure the success of the Hungarian Revolutionaries.

If indeed the Suez crisis stood in the way of the United Nations' intervention in Budapest, that was not the responsibility of the United Nations as such. It was the responsibility of certain of its members and their governments.

In all these matters we must search our consciences. In 1956 I listened to many critics of the United Nations, but I did not meet a father in that year or the next who was urging his government to send troops—to include his son—under the aegis of the United Nations across the Hungarian frontier. For these men would have been in the main American troops, British Commonwealth troops, and French troops; it is only through the forces of its members that the United Nations can wage war.

The Assembly, moreover, cannot demand that its members intervene in a given situation; it can only, through a majority, recommend that they do so, and the Security Council cannot intervene if the veto prevents it.

The United Nations has no greater powers than those conferred upon it by the Charter. If these powers are insufficient to save an invaded country, let us not blame the world organization. Let us rather work to improve and strengthen it, a task which will certainly involve some diminution of the national sovereignty of member states. Are we ready for that diminution? Are we ready to make the world organization a supraworld power, which at the present time it is not?

In answering these questions, to forget that the forces of

nationalism are still as strong as ever is mere wishful thinking, a dangerous basis for international policy. Many new states have gained independence since 1945 and jealously guard their sovereignty. More new states are to come. Only one state, Syria, has merged its sovereignty into a new united republic. None of the new states and few of the old have shown any enthusiasm for a permanent peace force, an indispensable requisite of a supraworld organization.

In saying this I am not pessimistic, for the United Nations through its members and its Secretary-General has many achievements to its credit. I simply plead for realism. Those who criticise the United Nations for a failure are really criticising its member governments. And in the majority of cases they are criticising themselves, for it is questionable whether the great body of critics of the United Nations are ready to give the organization supraworld powers.

Certainly the Communist world, stretching from the Iron Curtain to the Pacific, will not give the United Nations such powers.

The task of the members of the United Nations is to learn to use its power temperately, wisely and fairly, recognising all its limitations—and their own, a more difficult requisite.

I shall seek to show in these pages that even with these limitations, the United Nations, as an indispensable instrument for world order, can look back with satisfaction on its gains for peace and forward with hope for the promotion of political, physical, and social well-being throughout the world.

When the world organization is said to fail, dear reader, the fault lies rather with our governments and ourselves than with the United Nations.

CHAPTER I

The Parliament of Man

For I dipt into the future, far
    as human eye could see,
Saw the Vision of the world,
    and all the wonder that would be.
Saw the heavens fill with commerce,
    argosies of magic sails;
Pilots of the purple twilight,
    dropping down with costly bales;
Heard the heavens fill with shouting,
    and there rain'd a ghastly dew,
From the nation's airy navies
    grappling in the central blue,
Far along the world-wide whisper
    of the south-wind rushing warm,
With the standards of the people
    plunging thro' the thunder-storm;
Till the war drum throbbed no longer,
    and the battle flags were furled
In the Parliament of Man,
    the Federation of the world.

Locksley Hall (written in 1842).
Tennyson

IT IS 2:30 P.M. IN NEW YORK ON THE SECOND TUESDAY OF SEP-
tember outside the delegates' entrance to the United Nations.
The Assembly, our nearest but still hesitating and remote
approach to the Parliament of Man, will convene at 3:00 P.M.
to elect a new president, vice-presidents, and the chairmen of
seven committees.

The squat, white dreadnoughtlike edifice housing the Assembly is moored, as it were, near the East River, which
ripples and glistens as it flows by the Secretariat's towering
offices, shaped like a huge matchbox but transformed by the
sunshine's gleam on its marble and myriad windows.

Those who love an occasion are clustered in groups before
the delegates' entrance. There is expectancy as the great, the
near great, and those well known only in their own countries
—yet all aspiring to fame—arrive and look with becoming
modesty at the photographers. These cynical and pertinacious
gentlemen do not disappoint them. If the photograph will
not appear in the New York *Times,* there is always the chance
that it will be published back home in Europe, Asia, Latin
America, Africa, or the Western Pacific.

The outgoing President, who has held office for a year,
alights from his limousine. Photographers and movie men
press around him as he dutifully wreathes his face in the
smile now expected of a statesman or a politician, however
serious the moment and whatever his own particular feelings.

The outgoing President moves up the escalator, past the
Belgian mural on his left, largest in the world, past two great
Brazilian panels, one depicting man's lot in peace, the other
in war. This is indeed the appropriate theme of all striking
murals in the great modernistic buildings which are the home
of the United Nations.

The President now walks through the brown-carpeted lounge outside the great hall of the Assembly. He is widely greeted by his colleagues, convened from every country in the world save Communist China.

There is tall, thin, immaculately attired, rather stooped Krishna Menon with his inevitable walking stick, his dark eyes flashing as he holds court with Asians, Africans, and Europeans. Now he moves off to speak to the Russians, led a few years back by white-haired Andrei Vishinsky, his pale blue eyes peering through spectacles, eyes that had looked balefully at many an unhappy and doomed defendant. Now the Russian leader is Andrei Gromyko, short, dark, and dour but cordial enough as he shakes hands with Mr. Menon.

The President wends his way, now pausing to shake hands with Dr. Abdul Rahman of Malaya in his silken suit of many colours, with Ghanans in variegated and flowing robes, with Thor Thors, the courtly delegate from Iceland or with the veteran of them all, Abdullah Entezam of Iran, whose delicately chiselled, handsome features conceal a will of iron and a well-stored, mobile mind.

The President ascends to the thirty-eighth floor of the Secretariat, there to take possession of his suite for the last time. The thirty-eighth floor is justly famous. At the end of the long corridor and opposite the presidential suite are the quarters of the Secretary-General, Dag Hammarskjold, a chief source of power and influence in the United Nations. Here the skilful and scholarly Swede can sleep at night if his prolonged and devoted labours so require. He has at his disposal bedroom, bathroom, kitchen, dining room, conference room, and offices. The President, whose duties are not so continuous as those of the Secretary-General, is content with one large room and small adjoining quarters for his staff.

It is now nearly three. The President confers on the business of the day with Mr. Hammarskjold and with the latter's executive assistant, Andrew Cordier, formerly a professor of history and social sciences in the United States, knowledgeable in the ways of the Assembly where he has been a chief and influential official since its inception.

It is time to go down to the Assembly, first to the closely guarded and windowless offices behind the Hall, where the President, the Secretary-General, and Mr. Cordier each has a room and where one is likely to suffer from claustrophobia. There will be a contested election for the President's successor, and speculation is intense.

An official from Colombia and another from India are anxious that the President be ready for all emergencies. Will the incoming nominee get the necessary majority on the first ballot? Will the Russians raise the question of Chinese representation? Are all the delegates in their seats?

The moment has arrived. The President, the Secretary-General, and his executive assistant proceed to the dais. The floor of the Assembly is thronged with delegates, most of them milling around as they talk to their friends. Christian A. Herter and Henry Cabot Lodge of the United States are importuned by photographers to stand with Selwyn Lloyd, the Secretary of State for Foreign Affairs of the United Kingdom. The Russians are sitting imperturbably and inscrutably, waiting for the Assembly to begin.

Galleries are thronged. On the opening day of the session there is a fierce competition for seats. The ladies are there, too, and in a special place are the President's wife, Mrs. Henry Cabot Lodge, and other notables.

The President bangs his gavel. The photographers are finally, and with difficulty, persuaded to leave the Assembly, the delegates to take their seats, the voices to be stilled under the great dome until there is silence and the President declares the new session open and calls on all members to stand for a minute in silent prayer or in meditation, for the Communist members, it is believed, do not pray.

The pause is a long one; when you stand, a minute goes slowly. Incongruously and harshly, the silence is disturbed by the clicking of cameras from television booths.

The President resumes his seat and the Assembly proceeds to its first business, the election of the new President by secret ballot and without nomination. Counting votes takes some time, and there is a babble of conversation until the outgoing President announces that he has the honour of declaring his successor duly elected, who thereupon assumes the chair and delivers his speech of acceptance.

A new session of the General Assembly of the United Nations has begun. The world watches it with hope and with anxiety.

CHAPTER II

How the United Nations Works

> You may tell me that I have but to scan the present
> with realistic eyes in order to see these fine phrases
> often contemptuously reduced to a contemporary
> shambles . . . that some of the signatories to this
> Charter practice the opposite of what they preach
> even as they sign. . . . I reply that the nearer right
> you may be in any such gloomy indictment, the
> greater is the need for the new pattern which prom-
> ises at least to try to stem these evil tides . . . the
> greater becomes the importance of this self-denying
> ordinance, . . . the greater is the urgency for invoking
> the emancipations which the San Francisco Charter
> contemplates. If the effort fails, we can at least face
> the consequence with clean hands.
>
> Senator Arthur H. Vandenberg (1945)

I CEASED TO BE PRESIDENT OF THE ASSEMBLY ON SEPTEMBER 16,
1958, when I announced Dr. Charles Malik as my successor;
at that time he was Foreign Minister of the Lebanon. The
Chief of Protocol, the Comte de Noue, escorted me from the
dais to my place as head of the New Zealand delegation.

It was a time for reflection. I thought back to the days of
1945 in San Francisco, where both Senator Vandenberg and
Dr. Malik had taken an important part in drafting the Charter. But the thesis which was to shape its future had been

defined by Roosevelt, Churchill, and Stalin nearly a year before these two lesser figures became active.

The fundamental principle in the foundation of the United Nations was the assumption that the unity of Great Britain, the Soviet Union, and the United States would continue in peacetime. Often during the war this unity had been shaken, but with numerous and dangerous concessions to the Russians it continued throughout the world struggle. Today the tragedy is that this unity did not survive the war.

Field Marshal Smuts, in his anxiety to bring the Soviet Union into the proposed world organization wrote in September, 1944, to Mr. Churchill:

> On the merits, the principle of unanimity among the Great Powers has much to recommend it, at least for the years immediately following on this war. If this principle proves unworkable in practice, the situation could subsequently be reviewed when mutual confidence has been established and a more workable basis laid down. A clash at the present juncture should be avoided at all costs. In the event of unanimity for the Powers being adopted, even involving their voting on questions directly concerning their interests, the result will require that the United States and the United Kingdom should exert all their influence to get Russia to act moderately and sensibly and not to flout world opinion. And in this it is likely that they will be largely successful. Should Russia prove intransigent it may be necessary for the Organization to act, but the blame will attach to her. The principle of unanimity will at the worst only have the effect of a veto, of stopping action where it may be wise, or even necessary. Its effect will be negative; it will retard action. But it will also render it impossible for Russia to embark on courses not approved of by the United States and the United Kingdom.

Field Marshal Smuts did not defend the doctrine of unanimity among the Great Powers. In fact he disliked it but considered its acceptance inevitable.

Mr. Roosevelt's comment was illuminating. He thought it would be possible to accomplish the admission of the Soviet Union as a fully equal member of the new organization "by adjusting our differences through compromise by all the parties concerned and this ought to tide things over for a few years until the child learns how to toddle."

The child was born in 1945 at San Francisco when fifty governments agreed to the Charter; in October of that year these fifty, with the addition of Poland, established an international organization known as the United Nations.

Its membership has grown since then. With eighty-two members it now represents almost the entire world, save for Communist China which, with its 600,000,000 people, it must be admitted, is a sizeable chunk to be excluded.

The original signatories to the Charter expressed the hopes of a world painfully emerging from a holocaust:

We the peoples of the United Nations determined

to save succeeding generations from the scourge of war, which twice in our lifetime has brought sorrow to mankind; and to reaffirm faith in fundamental human rights, in the dignity and worth of the human person, in the equal rights of men and women and of nations large and small, and to establish conditions under which justice and respect for the obligations arising from treaties and other sources of international law can be maintained, and to promote social progress and better standards of life in larger freedom.

And for these ends

to practice tolerance and live together in peace with one another as good neighbors, and to unite our strength to maintain international peace and security, and to ensure, by the acceptance of principles and the institution of methods, that armed force shall not be used, save in the common interest, and to employ international machinery for the promotion of the economic and social advancement of all peoples,

have resolved to combine our efforts to accomplish these aims.

Year after year in the Security Council, in the Assembly, and in its committees I have heard one or another of the phrases of this exordium invoked by representatives of the member nations as they pleaded a cause.

All wish to save succeeding generations from the scourge of war. Yet progress toward disarmament is painfully slow in the nuclear age, when unlimited warfare would involve total destruction.

All reaffirm faith in fundamental human rights. Yet we witness denial of these rights from the iron to the bamboo curtain.

All at one time or another proclaim the sanctity of treaties. Yet the Russians repudiate their agreement on the status of Berlin.

All agree to practise tolerance and live together in peace with one another as good neighbours. Yet following 1945 the Soviet Union subverted one government after another in Eastern Europe, and subversion in the Middle East has been commonplace.

All agree to promote better standards of life. Yet the differences between developed and undeveloped nations are growing, not diminishing, and millions of people are still underfed and stricken by disease.

These are melancholy conclusions, but there is another side to the picture. After all, the United Nations is still young.

Under its aegis wars have been stopped in the Middle East, in Kashmir, and in Indonesia. Although there are no treaties of peace between Israel and the Arabs and although hostilities intermittently occur, there is no general war. A United Nations Emergency Force keeps peace in the Gaza Strip. There is an armistice in Korea. Through the farsighted generosity of the United States, through technical assistance rendered by the United Nations, and through the Colombo Plan much is being done to help the undeveloped countries.

Many new nations have arisen and entered the world organization. It is a place of immediate resort whenever peace is threatened. No government would dream of proposing its dissolution. Some misuse it, but all have recourse to it and seek to speak in its halls. "Better to jaw than to war." It is the chief debating organization of the world.

How does it work? Primarily the United Nations works through its six great organs or instruments: the General Assembly; the Security Council; the Economic and Social Council; the Trusteeship Council; the International Court of Justice; and the Secretariat, headed by the Secretary-General.

Whereas the General Assembly consists of all members of the United Nations, now expanded to eighty-two, the Security Council consists rigidly of only eleven, of which five— China, France, the Soviet Union, the United Kingdom, and the United States—are permanent members and the remainder are elected by the Assembly for a term of two years. Each of the permanent members has the right of veto; this veto, so constantly exercised by the Soviet Union, stultifies the capacity of the Council to act. The Soviet's indiscriminate use of the veto is the negation of the expectation that the unity of the Great Powers would extend from war to peace.

Although the Security Council has the primary responsibility for the maintenance of international peace and security, the General Assembly is empowered to consider—and does so in every regular session—the general principles of cooperation in the maintenance of international peace and security, including the principles governing disarmament and the regulation of armaments. The Assembly may make recommendations on these matters to the Security Council.

It is true, therefore, that there is competition between the Council as an executive body and the Assembly as a great forum for debate and recommendation. While the Security Council is exercising its functions in a particular matter, the Assembly can debate the problem but cannot make any recommendation unless the Council requests one. When the Assembly is in session, there is a growing tendency for member states to bypass the Council and initiate certain debates which more appropriately should have gone to the Council first.

I have always upheld the right of any state which genuinely sees a threat to its own or to international security to appeal to the United Nations. In these circumstances the Security Council has the right and the duty to act. The Assembly, moreover, has the right, subject to the limitations of domestic jurisdiction, to consider any situation which it deems likely to impair friendly relations among nations; but in the absence of a genuine threat to peace, public discussion of a dispute may exacerbate friendly relations and thus defeat its very purpose. There is a danger that the assertion of a virtually unlimited competence for the Assembly may weaken its influence; that to those against whom its unenforceable verdict is sought it will appear irresponsible; and that when that verdict fails to produce results, it will appear ineffective.

If this danger is to be avoided, the Assembly should not be used as a kind of court of first instance. Justifiable disputes, in particular, should be presented to the International Court of Justice which can exercise greater restraint and self-discipline, thereby avoiding a situation not contemplated by the founders of the organization: a situation in which the United Nations is used not as a centre for the composition of differences but as an arena for competitive propaganda and trials of strength among national and sectional interests.

Of the six instruments of the United Nations, normally only one can make decisions that bind the members of the organization—namely, the Security Council. But since any Great Power can veto a decision of the Council, its decisive power is severely limited.

The Assembly, save in a few instances, proceeds by way of recommendation to member states. Normally the Assembly does not and cannot legislate: it is far from being a Parliament of Man. On the contrary it constitutes the world's greatest forum for debate. In the Assembly there is no veto, although a two-third's majority is required in important matters.

As the Assembly sits for at least three months every year, and as from time to time it meets in emergency session, and as it is growing in power and influence, at the expense of the veto-ridden Security Council, I shall first discuss the working procedures of the Assembly. This is logical too, because the Assembly, with or without the conjunction of the Security Council, elects some or all members of the three Councils, the Judges of the International Court, and the Secretary-General.

As soon as the Assembly meets, it elects its new President, Vice-Presidents, and Chairmen of Committees. These elections are of significance because among other reasons the President, the eleven Vice-Presidents, and the seven Chairmen constitute what is known as the General Committee. In the very first days of the new session, this Committee recommends the items which should be inscribed on the agenda.

At one time, if the General Committee recommended against inscription, the Assembly would normally have followed the Committee's recommendation. But in recent years, with the addition of many new members from Africa and Asia, generally nourishing an anticolonial attitude, a recommendation against inclusion of an item having or appearing to have a colonial affiliation is likely to be swept aside in the Assembly. Consider Indonesia's claiming from the Dutch the territory which is known as Netherlands New Guinea but which the Indonesians prefer to call West Irian. At one time it was conceivable that the General Committee would have voted against inscribing on the agenda an item involving the Indonesian claim to this territory. Today, even if there were a Committee vote against inscription, the Assembly would in all probability reverse the recommendation. The tendency is for a majority to favour the discussion of any and every item.

By custom, each of the five Great Powers—the United States, the United Kingdom, the Soviet Union, France, and China—provides a Vice-President. He is not elected by name but by country, and consequently the senior representative of his country functions as a Vice-President. The United States, the United Kingdom, the Soviet Union, and France never have any difficulty in being elected. But in recent years China, represented by the government in Taiwan, is being elected by a narrowing margin.

The other six Vice-Presidents come from smaller powers. These positions are eagerly sought, both for prestige and for membership on the General Committee. The President may, if he chooses, depute the chairmanship of an assembly meeting to a Vice-President. I did this infrequently and only for brief periods.

Usually after much lobbying before the Session, the list of Vice-Presidents and Chairmen of Committees is arranged before the opening day and voting is then in most cases a formality. By custom, and I think wisely, no chairman is a citizen of one of the Great Powers. No representative of a satellite has been elected chairman of either of the two political committees.

On the opening day the Assembly resolves itself into each of its committees and proceeds with the formality of electing the seven chairmen. The choice of each chairman is important, for he has the responsibility of guiding the debate in his respective committee and ensuring that the work of his committee is completed with expedition so that the Assembly can wind up its business by the appointed day before Christmas. Achieving this goal is helped by the anxiety of diplomats to get home before Christmas.

All these elections out of the way, the Assembly proceeds to the general debate. But, although thus described, it is not a debate in the Parliamentary sense, with members speaking from their seats and engaging in the cut-and-thrust of argument. Each representative of his country, whether he be a Foreign Minister or of lesser rank, reads from the rostrum a set speech, often prepared in his capital and enunciating his government's policy on all the important issues. Very few representatives speak *ex tempore* and certainly none from the Great Powers. There is little oratory save from one or two Latin Americans. The only European that I have heard in the Assembly who had the qualities of oratory was Paul-Henri Spaak of Belgium. But when he speaks from a few notes, as he did in a great speech in the Commemorative Assembly in San Francisco in 1955, he has little chance of being adequately reported. Journalists today like a complete text. Spontaneous oratory too often does not reach the world.

Thus in the general debate, the Assembly—and the world—hears grand and prepared declarations of policy on momentous subjects from Christian R. Herter, Selwyn Lloyd, Andrei Gromyko, Maurice Couve de Murville of France, John Diefenbaker, and Sir Pierson Dixon to mention only a few.

When these gentlemen speak in the general debate, the galleries are full, television lights shine mercilessly on the speaker, and the world both hears and sees "diplomacy by television." It is a measure of the Assembly's importance that these eminent makers of policy attend its deliberations. Some foreign ministers may be critical of the Assembly—and in private discussion often are—but even these feel obliged to be present and to speak.

In the Assembly sit the representatives of eighty-two member-nations from great to small. Each member has a Mission in New York, headed by a diplomat called the "permanent representative" of his country to the United Nations and holding, therefore, the rank and the title of Ambassador.

This Chief of Mission attends to the day-to-day matters of his country's relations with the United Nations and its various subsidiary bodies. The permanent representative, who is normally a trained (or career) diplomat, may, of course, be a woman. For instance, Sweden's permanent representative is the able and charming Mrs. Agda Rossel.

When the Assembly meets, the chairman and leader of his country's delegation is not necessarily the permanent representative. That is a matter for his government. Generally speaking, and at least for some time during the early days of an Assembly Session, governments are represented by their foreign ministers, who while in New York lead their delegations. When they depart, a junior minister of a Great Power may lead the delegation or in the case of the smaller nations, the permanent representative will take over. But custom varies.

Consider the United Kingdom. Two or three days before the session opens, a Minister of State will come to New York from London. He is not a member of the British Cabinet but he is a politician of experience enjoying the confidence of the British Foreign Secretary. The Foreign Secretary will probably arrive shortly after the session commences, stay to deliver a speech in the general debate and remain for some days afterward, then return to his pressing Parliamentary duties in London and the day-to-day control of the Foreign Office in Downing Street. The Minister of State remains to the end of the session.

Normally the Secretary of State of the United States will deliver the first or at least the second speech in the general debate. He represents the host country and also the most powerful state in the world, which looks to him. So far as Mr. Herter's manifold duties in Washington and elsewhere permit him, he will stay for some time during the general debate and in particular listen to the speeches of the foreign ministers of the United Kingdom, France, the Soviet Union, and Canada, whose moral influence is scarcely less than that of a Great Power. If the President of the Assembly is a student of psychology, as he normally is, he will enjoy watching the faces of the various leading foreign ministers as they listen to their colleagues. Many have a remarkable gift, under such circumstances, of appearing as if nothing important is happening. When the Secretary of State leaves, the permanent representative, Henry Cabot Lodge, takes over.

The last speaker in the general debate is Krishna Menon of India. He has no inherent title to this position, but to either the amusement or the chagrin of his audience he invariably secures it, thus enabling him to survey the world, traverse the speeches of those he thinks worthy of his attention (and many escape the honour), and deliver the ultimate wisdom on every subject. He has copious notes which he frequently mislays. His walking stick is beside him, precariously suspended from the tribune. Sometimes he gets tired, draws his hand in distraught fashion through his distinguished mop of hair, but however tired, however nervy, he speaks for at least two hours and every delegate is present to listen to him. He is oracular and does not hesitate to lecture his associates, as when he told the First Committee that he thought his colleagues had been "thinking aloud but more aloud than thinking." But make no mistake about it: Mr. Menon is a man of great ability and influence and he is heard with the closest attention.

Before the general debate is concluded, the work of the committees has begun. But the First Committee, which deals with the great political issues of the day, never commences its deliberations until the general debate is over.

All seven committees are committees of the whole. Each is therefore a miniature assembly. Every member state has a seat on each committee. It may readily be seen what a strain on personnel this imposes on the smaller states. To the Great Powers, with their formidable array of politicians and trained personnel, this is no problem. But some of the smaller nations have to switch a representative from one committee to another, and often seats are vacant.

Generally speaking, all items on the agenda are first dealt with in one or another of the committees whose functions are thus divided:

The First Committee will consider great political problems such as disarmament, the control of outer space, the unification of Korea, the future of Algeria and of Cyprus.

The Special Political Committee will consider such problems as those of the relief of the Arab Refugees, the question of amendments to the Charter (which in any case cannot be altered without the authority of two-thirds of the Assembly and consent of all permanent members of the Security Council), the treatment of Indians in the Union of South Africa and Apartheid (or the legislation affecting the native inhabitants of South Africa).

The Second Committee deals with economic matters and the question of assistance to undeveloped countries of the world.

The responsibility of the Third Committee is the consideration of human rights.

The Fourth Committee deals with colonial questions and

the advancement toward self-government of the Trusteeship and other nonself-governing territories.

The Fifth Committee settles the budget of the United Nations and its administrative problems.

The Sixth Committee considers the multifarious legal problems confronting the United Nations, such as the law of the sea and the definition of aggression.

Each committee will make its recommendations in the form of draft resolutions. After they are passed—and only a bare majority is necessary—they come before the Assembly which approves of them or not, as it thinks fit. If a resolution deals with a matter of "importance" it cannot be adopted in the Assembly unless it receives a two-thirds' majority of the members present and voting. This necessity for a two-thirds' majority, in comparison to a simple majority in a committee, may be irksome to some but not nearly so irksome as the veto in the Security Council. Some matters of "importance" are defined by the Charter; others are declared to be of "importance" by a simple majority of the Assembly.

Those matters defined as "important" by the Charter are:

1. recommendations with respect to the maintenance of international peace and security;
2. the election of
    a. the nonpermanent members of the Security Council;
    b. the members of the Economic and Social Council;
    c. the nonpermanent members of the Trusteeship Council;
3. the admission of new members to the United Nations; but applicants for admission first have to run the gauntlet of the veto in the Security Council;

4. the suspension of the rights and privileges of membership;
5. the expulsion of members;
6. questions relating to the operation of the trusteeship system (under which member states are trustees for peoples not yet self-governing) and budgetary questions. Thus the question of how the United Nations Emergency Force in the Gaza Strip was to be paid for was an "important" item.

Not all matters go to a committee. Sometimes, particularly when a Special Assembly is convened, the Assembly will tend to deal with a problem itself without any reference to a committee. Thus when I presided over the Third Emergency Session in August, 1958, the Assembly itself dealt throughout with the items concerning disturbed conditions in Lebanon and Jordan. Then indeed the Assembly became the grand inquest for the world.

CHAPTER III

Limitations of the Assembly

SINCE ENTERING THE UNITED NATIONS IN 1955 THE IRISH HAVE
been represented by colourful and effective figures who have
a natural flair for oratory. Frank Aiken, Eire's Minister of External Affairs, and Frederick Boland, the Irish permanent
representative to the United Nations, always win close attention in debate, even though Mr. Aiken's proposals for Western disengagement from Europe and Soviet retirement from
the satellites earned this Catholic statesman applause mainly
from the Communist bloc and the neutralists.

His assertion that we have no third party in the present
division of mankind except the collective judgment of mankind represented in the Assembly drew considerable acclaim.
Yet it always must be remembered that, in the words of Mr.
Hammarskjold, "The Charter, read as a whole, does not
endow the United Nations with any of the attributes of a
superstate or of a body active outside the framework of decisions of member governments."

Too many in a situation such as the crushing of the Hungarian revolution in 1956 by the Soviet are ready to say that
the United Nations failed to save the Hungarian people, as
if the world organization were a political entity separate from
its member governments and able to act independently of
their decisions. This is a misleading concept.

Again, to paraphrase Mr. Hammarskjold, the world organization is rather an instrument for negotiation *among* and, to some extent, *for* governments. If member governments fail to use this instrument, that is their responsibility. It is not the responsibility or the fault of the United Nations.

In 1956 and 1957 the Russians were ready enough to upbraid the British, the French, and the Israelis because they did not at once observe the recommendations of the Assembly and immediately withdraw their forces from Egyptian territory. But when the Assembly urged the Russians to withdraw their forces from Hungary, the Soviet government saw the matter in another light.

In one of his letters to President Eisenhower, Marshal Bulganin had this to say:

> The United Nations is not a kind of world government adopting laws and decisions binding on all states. When the United Nations was being organised, it was intended, and this is very clearly set forth in the Charter, that the states should become its members voluntarily and voluntarily undertake obligations to fulfil the provisions of the Charter while fully retaining their independence of action.

Further on in his letter the former Soviet Prime Minister asks:

> Can it be forgotten that United Nations member states are sovereign and independent states and cannot brook the imposition of decisions incompatible with their sovereignty?

I recall a comment by the Canadian statesman, Lester Pearson, who said that we must never forget that:

> The Assembly cannot order anybody to do anything. Its votes are only recommendations and therefore in that sense

are not as important as those of a national parliament. People become disillusioned when recommendations, which they confuse with orders, are not carried out; or, even worse, carried out only in certain circumstances.

I refer elsewhere to certain legislative or perhaps quasi-legislative powers which the Assembly appears to possess. This aspect of the Assembly's functions is not mentioned in the above statements. But the point I would emphasise is that there are definite and recognised limitations on the legal powers of the United Nations. At the same time, its importance as a touchstone of national policy should not be overlooked.

I might illustrate what the United Nations legally is not and what morally it is, by referring to the various resolutions passed in 1956 and 1957 with respect to the crises which arose in the Middle East and in Hungary. I do not intend to rehearse the reasons adduced in the United Nations as to why Israeli forces staged a large-scale incursion into Egyptian territory or why the United Kingdom and France intervened to separate the combatants. Nor shall I discuss the justifications advanced by the Soviet Union for the action it took to crush the national revolution in Hungary. In my judgment the three actions should be evaluated separately.

What is of direct relevance, however, is the fact that the great majority of United Nations members believed that none of these actions could derive legal or moral sanction from the Charter. The Assembly passed resolutions calling on the forces concerned to withdraw from the territories to which they had been dispatched. All these resolutions were recommendations. They could not be enforced against the will of those to whom they were addressed. Nevertheless, Britain and

France withdrew with a minimum of delay. Israel withdrew the last of its troops late in February, 1957, a little over three months after their first penetration into Egypt. The United Kingdom, France, and Israel withdrew, not because the resolutions adopted by the Assembly were legally binding on them but because, among other reasons, those resolutions reflected the feeling of a great body of world public opinion. The three governments concerned did not ignore the disapprobation expressed by so large a part of the international community.

In the case of Hungary, however, the Soviet Union, from the beginning, refused to heed either the Assembly's resolutions condemning Russian action or its demand that the Russians withdraw their troops from Hungary. It might be mentioned that the Assembly did not act to condemn the United Kingdom, France, or Israel. Nor did any of its resolutions charge them with aggression, as in the case of the Soviet Union's attack on the Hungarians. When Israel delayed its withdrawal from the Gaza Strip and the Sharm el Sheikh area in the Straits of Aqaba, a resolution proposing the application of sanctions was introduced, but no formal action was taken to have the Assembly vote on it.

The compliance of the United Kingdom and France, and eventually of Israel, with the political recommendations of the Assembly stands out in sharp contrast to the refusal of the Soviet Union to be deflected from its chosen course. There was considerable public and diplomatic discussion about what might be done to secure Moscow's compliance with the wishes of the United Nations. But, as Mr. Pearson has cogently pointed out, if the opponents of the Soviet action had intervened by force in Hungary through the United Nations, the first victims would have been the Hungarians themselves, and the rest of the world might have followed them into the abyss.

One comment on the political implications for the United Nations concerning the Suez and Hungarian crises: it is my belief that no Great Power—and I use the term "Great" here only in its physical sense—can expect to act entirely at its own discretion, heedless of condemnation and openly in contempt of the public conscience of the world; no Great Power, I repeat, can indulge in this sort of behaviour as one Great Power has done, and expect that there will be no impairment of confidence either in its own probity or in the capacity of the United Nations to preserve peace with justice. The exercise of lawless violence and a refusal to withdraw from advantages secured by it can only diminish the stature and the authority of the Charter. Those who bear great responsibilities should be the first to deny that national expediency can ever justify a deliberate departure from the imperatives of the Charter. Those who breach the Charter and who not only refuse to repair that breach but also seek to lay blame on others for the consequence are adding to the sin of tyranny, which is the abuse of strength, the no less reprehensible sin of hypocrisy.

This may seem a harsh judgment on my part. But the Charter allows no other to be reached. It does not, however, alter the truth of the observation made by the Secretary-General in his "Report to the Twelfth Assembly" that:

> If properly used, the United Nations can serve a diplomacy of reconciliation better than other instruments available to member states.

With Mr. Hammarskjold, I believe also that:

> To turn aside from the United Nations now because it cannot be transformed into a world authority enforcing the law upon the nations would be to erase all the steady, though slow and painful, advances that have been made and to close the door to hopes for the future of world society toward which present efforts and experience should be at least a modest stepping stone.

In relation to Hungary, the United Nations has been able to achieve little, other than to record the moral indignation felt throughout the world. The conclusion to be drawn from this is that where a Great Power, like the Soviet Union, is not prepared to co-operate with the world organization, the United Nations cannot take effective action unless other Great Powers are prepared to impose sanctions or perhaps even to risk a world war. The central feature in the Hungarian crisis is that the United States, Great Britain, and other Western Powers were not prepared to risk war with the Soviet, an understandable reluctance which prevented the United Nations from achieving any solution.

Britain and France were stopped, by Great Power pressure in the United Nations, from completing a police action against Egypt, an action which the United Nations itself had been unready to perform initially. The great and beneficial result of the Anglo-French action is that the United Nations has now interposed its own police force, a step which Sir Anthony Eden had desired from the outset. He had declared that the United Kingdom was ready and willing to give way to the United Nations in Egypt as soon as the world organization was ready and willing to undertake responsibility.

We have reached the position, if the arguments of the

critics of Britain and France are true, that however imminent and serious the danger, no power, except in self-defence, can use force to protect its vital interests and to preserve the peace, save with the consent of the Security Council and therefore of Russia. If that consent is not forthcoming, then only with the consent of two-thirds of the Assembly.

In great degree, the power of the Assembly depends on its capacity to bring to bear the force of moral opinion. But the force of world moral opinion is likely to be effective only in countries within which domestic moral opinion may develop. This applies to Britain and France but has no relevance to the Soviet Union where domestic moral opinion appears to have little impact.

There is thus this conclusion: the United Nations is not of itself a substitute for power. Resolutions which are not backed by force or the fear of force or by economic pressures will not change the course of history. Certainly they will not redress the wrongs of an oppressed people, as in Hungary.

The Assembly of the United Nations succeeded in persuading Britain and France to accede to its recommendations primarily, if not only, because two Great Powers backed these recommendations and, in the case of the United States, declined to proceed with steps to remedy Europe's desperate oil situation until there was satisfactory evidence of the intention to withdraw Anglo-French troops from Egypt.

Following the downfall of the French monarchy, Burke wrote that we should "make the Revolution a parent of settlement and not a nursery of future revolutions." It was not until the Congress of Vienna that settlements of some durability were produced. It is the task of the United Nations, confronted by revolutionary processes in the Middle East, to complete the job it has begun, to see that the United Nations Emergency Force remains in the area until there is a final settlement of Arab-Israeli relations. If the world organizations does less, it will not have made its resolutions with respect to Britain and France a parent of settlement; it will, to vary the metaphor, have permitted the soil of the Middle East to produce an even greater crop of troubles to plague the area and the world. Fortunately the Egyptian government appears content to leave the UNEF where it is: a wise decision.

In spite of the setbacks experienced by the Assembly, all of us must have been struck by the increase in its political status, an increase owing in large measure to the decline in the power and the influence of the Security Council because of the Soviet veto. Although the Charter invests the Council with the "primary responsibility for the maintenance of international peace and security" and, indeed, gives it power to make binding orders as distinct from the recommendations which may be adopted by the Assembly, the course of events since 1945 has shorn the Council of much of its real authority. It has never had military units at its disposal for the enforcement of its decisions. Under Articles 43 and 45 in Chapter VII of the Charter, member states were to make these units available. Its intervention in Korea in 1950 was possible only because, at the crucial time, the Soviet Union absented itself from the Council. Even in this case the Council proceeded by recommendation and not by order.

It is significant too, that, aware of the Council's limitations and its inability to act if the veto were used, the Assembly subsequently, in November, 1950, established the Uniting for Peace procedure, under which it dealt with the Suez and

Hungarian crises. The terms of the relevant part of the Uniting for Peace Resolution merit enunciation.

The Assembly resolved that if the Security Council, because of the lack of unanimity of its permanent members, failed to exercise its primary responsibility for the maintenance of international peace and security in any case where there appeared to be a threat to the peace, breach of the peace, or act of aggression, then the Assembly should consider the matter immediately with a view to making appropriate recommendations to members for collective measures. These measures were to include, in the case of a breach of the peace or act of aggression, the use of armed force, when necessary, to maintain or restore international peace and security. If the Assembly were not in session at the time, then it would meet in special emergency session within twenty-four hours from the time it was requested to do so. Such session would be called if requested by the Security Council on the vote of any seven members, or by a majority of the members of the United Nations. This procedure was not used until 1956, following the Suez and Hungarian crises. It is one of the ironies of history that the Uniting for Peace procedure should have been invoked first against two such liberty-loving nations as the British and the French and that the Russians, who had previously declared the procedure to be illegal, should have cheerfully voted for its use in the Suez crisis.

For a man in my position as the permanent representative of New Zealand those were dark days. In terms of kinship, affection, and interest no country is closer to the United Kingdom than mine. My government had decided to support the United Kingdom in its intervention in Egypt, believing it to be a police action to preserve the peace in the Middle East. Anxiously I had followed the Security Council debates after the Anglo-French landings and had heard the British and the French exercise the veto, which made inevitable an immediate meeting of the Assembly under the Uniting for Peace procedure. In invoking this procedure the representatives of the United States and the Soviet Union perforce moved together.

When that fateful Assembly met, I did not speak until about two in the morning. Earlier amid general uproar and excitement an attempt had been made to move the closure, and only after an indignant protest was I able to secure the right to be heard. Of course the outcome was a foregone conclusion: by an overwhelming majority the British, the French, and the Israelis were called upon to withdraw.

It was after the vote that Lester Pearson made his historic proposal for the creation of a United Nations Emergency Force, which would supervise the withdrawal of the intervening forces from the Canal Zone and the Sinai peninsula. These forces are now in the Gaza Strip and the area of Sharm el Sheikh. Such a proposal was not new. A similar one had been made by the New Zealand representative in 1947 when he suggested that Jerusalem should be neutralised and its neutrality maintained by a United Nations force, to which my country offered to contribute, but the suggestion went unheeded.

I have already mentioned Lester Pearson's view that the Assembly cannot order anybody to do anything. It is quite true that in San Francisco in 1945 only the Philippines voted for its own proposal that the Assembly be authorised "to enact rules of international law which should become binding on members after such rules shall have been approved by the Security Council." However, it has been pointed out that the Assembly may clearly determine with legal effect questions relating to its own procedure or the internal organization and the finance of the United Nations and to its own relations with other sections of that body.

Let me refer to the decisions of the Twelfth Assembly to continue the United Nations Emergency Force in the Middle East. UNEF has achieved a most heartening degree of success in maintaining stability and calm on the Egyptian-Israeli frontier, an area long the scene of violence and bloodshed. By agreeing in principle to apportion the costs of the Emergency Force among its membership, the Assembly placed a welcome emphasis on the concept of collective responsibility. I think that there is sound argument, as well, for the thesis that in this case the Assembly acted in a legislative sense.

The Assembly, by a resolution passed on November 22, 1957, authorised the Secretary General to expend for the period ending December 31, 1957, an amount up to a maximum of $30 million and, as necessary, an amount for the continuing operation of the Force beyond that date up to a maximum of $25 million, subject to any decisions on a review. The Assembly went on—and I quote from its resolution—to "decide" that the expenses thus authorised "shall be borne by the members of the United Nations in accordance with the scale of assessments adopted by the General Assembly for the financial years 1957 and 1958 respectively."

It is true that the Communist bloc and Chile and Ecuador voted against this resolution and that the Communist countries, whose contributions to the regular United Nations budget amount to 20 per cent of the total, said that they would not contribute their share to UNEF expenses. But I am of the opinion that the resolution is binding on all members of the United Nations. Its legal effect will, in the minds of some, I realise, be debatable, especially since the members of the Communist bloc have said so uncompromisingly that the resolution is not binding on them, that the "aggressors" alone should pay. Of course Britain, France, and Israel have not been defined as aggressors by the Assembly. It appears to me that since the Charter provides simply that "the expenses of the Organization shall be borne by the members as apportioned by the General Assembly," a member's failure to pay its due proportion of the expenses of the United Nations Emergency Force will eventually involve the consequences referred to in Article 19, whereby a member in arrears in the payments of its financial contributions to the Organization shall have no vote in the Assembly if the amount of its arrears equals or exceeds the amount of the contributions due from it for the preceding two years.

CHAPTER IV

Drama in the Security Council

A MEETING OF THE SECURITY COUNCIL IS ABOUT TO BEGIN. Delegates and their staffs are gathering in a small lounge from which the Press is excluded. They are discussing procedures to be followed and substantive steps to be taken. As usual, the representatives of the smaller powers are seeking information from the staffs of the American and British delegations.

The President has a special room, and during my terms I found it to be a busy centre of activity. If the meeting was to start at 3:00 P.M. I invariably tried, amid all my preoccupations, to be in my room at least twenty minutes earlier, available for consultations with delegations and the Secretariat. Sometimes, anxiously keeping one eye on the clock, I held urgent private meetings. The Secretariat official generally advising me was Dr. Dragon Protitch, a skilled and experienced Yugoslav and a loyal and impartial friend. As a supporter of the dignity of my office, he never summoned me to the Chamber to assume the chair until all the delegates had been seated.

On great occasions I felt the drama of it all. As I entered, the Council room was abuzz with conversation and still filled with photographers and reporters. Behind me, as I took my seat, was a mural depicting man's painful ascent from slavery

45

and war to the plains of peace where men and women of all races freely mingled. I looked around, saw that the Press withdrew, banged my gavel and called the Council to order. Suddenly all was hushed. The Council proceeded to adopt its agenda and enter upon its grave deliberations.

In 1954 and 1955 I represented New Zealand on the Security Council, my country's only term of office in this august body. There had been earlier periods when the Council appeared to have become almost moribund; governments were reluctant to resort to an organ so constantly stultified by Russia's veto. But in the latter part of 1953, with subjects as diverse as the future of Trieste and the bitter Arab-Israeli controversy, the Council seemed to gain a new lease on life. I sought to prepare myself for a busy two years.

In each calendar month the Council sits under a different President, the rotation proceeding by the initial letter of the name of each member. Technically it is the country, not its delegate, which is President. For January, 1954, the President was Lebanon, whose delegation, headed by Dr. Charles Malik, therefore provided the person occupying the chair. New Zealand was to follow in February.

The dispute occupying the attention of the Council in January arose out of an important Arab-Israeli incident. By the Council's rules a President, when his country is concerned in a dispute, can vacate the chair and request the next member in rotation to assume the office. At the last moment Dr. Malik decided to do this, and on the first day I sat in the Council I had the responsibility of the presidential office.

The President settles the list of speakers and rules on points of order. Since there are procedural wrangles, often taking considerable time, he must have an intimate knowledge of the rules. The arguments over procedure, boring as they may seem to the public, are often important. Thus proposals for priority, if carried, frequently give the successful member the initiative in the debate and the right to secure a first vote on its proposal.

The President of the Council, unlike the President of the Assembly, sits in a dual capacity, first as the President and secondly as the representative of his country. When he decides to speak as representative, he announces that he will do so in this capacity. He can do this at any time in the debate, although usually by custom he will speak at the end of the debate. While President, Yakov A. Malik of the Soviet Union, not to be confused with Dr. Charles Malik of the Lebanon, did not hesitate constantly to intervene on behalf of the Soviet Union.

In 1950 the Russian delegation boycotted the Security Council for six months. Their absence that June enabled the Council, unhindered by a Soviet veto, to pass its celebrated resolution calling upon member states to assist in repelling aggression in Korea. Even the Russians can make mistakes. In August, 1950, it was the Russian turn for the Presidency and their delegation suddenly returned, led by the redoubtable Yakov Malik. Of his conduct as President, Trygve Lie makes this pungent comment in his book *In the Cause of Peace:* "Mr. Malik indeed returned and launched a month of misuse of his powers, in an attempt to bog down the Council's Korean action." Fortunately he failed. The point is that a President, if he wishes to debase his office, has ample opportunities.

During New Zealand's term in the Security Council, Andrei Vishinsky generally represented Russia and I am bound to say that he did not misuse his powers when he sat as President. Nobody will be surprised when I write that there is always considerable manoeuvring to bring an item before the Council when the Chair is occupied by a person who will proceed impartially.

During the first of my three one-month terms as President I undertook to confine the debate to a particular item and to rule out of order any reference to another item on the agenda. This was not easy. A delegate may enter a forbidden field, and by the time he is interrupted he has made his point. I avoided this by reading in advance copies of speeches which delegates proposed to make. If one touched on the forbidden topic, I interrupted and with all courtesy and firmness asked the speaker not to read the offending portion. My request was heeded. This was the first and really the only occasion when Mr. Vishinsky raised his eyebrows against any ruling of mine. He suggested, in surprisingly moderate terms, that my procedure was unorthodox. But he did not attempt to reverse me.

The calibre of the work of delegates in the Security Council is very high. A foreign minister of a member can attend at any time. Thus in the Suez debate the United States, Britain, and France were frequently represented by their foreign ministers. I do not need to emphasise the capacity of men such as the late John Foster Dulles, Selwyn Lloyd, and Christian Pineau. Statesmen like these are assisted by expert staffs and their speeches are delivered only after meticulous preparation by experienced hands.

It has always been a source of pride to me that New Zealand, during its term on the Council, with a staff so much smaller than that available to a Great Power, made contributions that could be compared to those of any other member.

My government had two important responsibilities: first the initiation and conduct of a proposal to the Security Council that Egypt should cease its blockade of the Suez Canal against Israel, and later the launching of an item in the Council having as its object "the cessation of hostilities in the area of the offshore islands." The responsibility of steering both these proposals through the Council was mine.

Of course these proposals were the result of prolonged consultations between the Western Great Powers and the country taking the initiative, in this case New Zealand. Much took place before a letter from the New Zealand permanent representative, requesting a meeting of the Council, was lodged with the Secretary-General. Before the meeting, Mr. Hammarskjold and all members of the Council were informed of the initiative.

The proposal for the cessation of the Egyptian blockade had its elements of drama. The gallery was always packed. The New York public seems fascinated by proceedings in the Council, particularly where the Middle East is involved. The delegates are almost in a goldfish bowl, their every gesture watched. The Russians attract particular attention and when, as President, I called on Mr. Vishinsky, there was always an excited whispering of his name, a susurration among the spectators.

During the debate, bitter as it was between Egypt and Israel, the Egyptian delegate attracted much attention by his quaint wit and gesticulations. I was informed that he had been married to a Jewess whom he had loved dearly and who had died some time back. Late one afternoon his speech became very deliberate, then halting. At the time I thought that this was all part of the peculiar mode of address he had chosen. Suddenly he ceased to speak, his hand clutched at a glass of water, his shoulders huddled and drooped, his head fell slowly to the desk. It was no act. He was dying, and in irony of fate a Jewish doctor of the Israeli delegation rushed to his side and pronounced him dead.

Nobody was sure until the vote came on the resolution that the blockade of the Canal against Israel should cease, whether Mr. Vishinsky would veto the New Zealand proposal. Some years before, when a vote on a similar proposal took place, the Soviet had abstained. This time, with a wicked illogicality which did not in the least embarrass him, Mr. Vishinsky cast the veto. It was my first experience with this stultification by the Russians. The British representative, Sir Gladwyn Jebb, a master of irony and invective, delivered a withering denunciation of the Russian negative veto. Mr. Vishinsky took it all very calmly, adopting an attitude of injured innocence, a role which did not suit him. The Charter, he said, gave permanent members the right to veto. Why, then, complain of its use. If Russia had cast the veto so many times, that in Mr. Vishinsky's view only proved her always right.

The next item in which New Zealand took the initiative concerned the offshore islands. These proceedings, launched on January 31, 1955, have a relevance for the present day. Beginning in September, 1954, and continuing into 1955 the Chinese Communists intermittently conducted a series of artillery bombardments against the Quemoys and the Matsus, with dire threats against Formosa. The Nationalist Chinese evacuated some small islands called the Tachens, but they were resolute to remain in the Quemoys and the Matsus.

They have continued to remain there and have considerably augmented their forces.

New Zealand's aim was to stop the shooting, and the proposed proceedings were kept a close secret. Although consultations were carried on for months in Washington and New York, not a word leaked out until in a morning of hectic interviews late in January, 1955, I informed all the members of the Council, including the Soviet representative, of my government's proposals. It is a queer experience to enter the silent and rather depressing offices of the Russian delegation on Park Avenue, where Arkady Sobolev received me upstairs with his usual noncommittal courtesy. As I was informing him of our initiative, the British Ambassador in Moscow on New Zealand's behalf was communicating the news to the Kremlin. All was done on a rigid timetable.

Later in the same day I held a press conference. I was careful to confine the discussion to our objective which was to stop the fighting and prevent its extension into a wider conflagration. I emphasised a point which is still true, that fighting a seemingly remote place of the world can spread like a fire to burn all. I declined to be drawn into any discussion of the recognition of Communist China or of Communist China's claim to the seat in the United Nations occupied by the Republic of China.

The Council met at my request as a result of a letter which I addressed to myself as its President, concluding with the usual form of words in which I asked myself as President to accept "the assurances of my highest consideration" from myself as New Zealand's permanent representative: a formula which caused some amusement in New York.

The Chinese Communists were invited to attend a meeting

of the Council. They never accepted the invitation; the Council did not discuss the matter further, and seemingly its proceedings were abortive. Nonetheless I believe they had some effect. The initial debate was widely televised and of course more widely reported. It served notice on the Communist world of the gravity attached by the democracies to the attempt by the Chinese Communists to seize the offshore islands, reinforced, too, by the resolution of Congress empowering the President to take such military action as might be required, including action against the mainland, if the concentration of Chinese troops there was such as to constitute an immediate threat against Formosa.

In fact, the threatened attack on Quemoy did not materialise. The late Mr. Dulles attributed this to the warning that the United States, though not directly involved, was prepared to use force in defence of its vital interests and for the maintenance of peace. I am also prepared to give some credit to the influence of the Security Council and perhaps, too, to the restraining influence of the Soviet in Peking. I am in doubt whether the Kremlin wishes to be dragged into war on the heels of the Chinese. Not until August, 1958, following the Assembly's success in relaxing tension in the Middle East, did the Chinese Communists resume a massive artillery bombardment of Quemoy. The timing was significant and sinister, but the Communists have not yet attempted a landing on Quemoy.

The New Zealand item in respect to the offshore islands is still on the agenda of the Security Council and could be revived if the Central People's Republic of China attempted to land its forces on the islands. The difficulty is that the Council, in such a case, would probably be unable, because of the veto, to invoke the use of force against the aggressor and the Assembly could act only slowly. It seems clear that the United States would not wait for the United Nations if Formosa's security were involved. The President, in his message to Congress on January 24, 1955, said that the situation had become sufficiently critical to compel him, "without awaiting action by the United Nations, to ask Congress to participate now by specific resolution in measures designed to improve measures for peace."

Professor A. L. Goodhart, a well-known American authority on international law and Master of University College, Oxford, considered, during the Suez crisis of 1956 when Britain and France intervened in Egypt, that their action had some analogy to the President's proposals in respect to Quemoy. The Professor said that the seizure of the Canal by Colonel Nasser constituted a threat to the British and French interests more immediate than the American interest in Quemoy and was also a threat to Israel, which the Colonel had planned to destroy. "In these circumstances," the Professor pointed out, "it would not have been surprising if direct action had been taken, but the London Conference, by a large majority, decided to negotiate with Nasser."

The intransigence of Egypt made any settlement impossible after reference to the United Nations and was followed by repeated Egyptian infiltration over the Israel border, the Jordan elections, and Jordan-Egyptian military alliance. "Whether strictly legal or not, Israeli retaliation can hardly have been unexpected," states Professor Goodhart.

"In these circumstances, what steps should Great Britain have taken?" he asks. "An easy answer would have been to join in appeal to the United Nations, but as in the case of

Quemoy the situation was too critical to await action by the Security Council for there was a strong risk that, if there was any delay, war between Israel and Egypt would spread throughout the Middle East. This threat has been successfully met."

The Professor concludes: "Now it will be possible, after fighting has ceased, to deal with the problem as a whole. Finally, there is hope that a United Nations police force, with power to guarantee order, will be established. It will then become clear that the United Nations has been transformed from a society which in the past have proved to be largely ineffective into an efficient machine for the maintenance of peace."

In my view, Professor Goodhart's observations in relation to Quemoy give valuable perspective to the action taken in Egypt by the United Kingdom and France.

The smaller countries set great store by their right to resort to the Security Council. During New Zealand's term on the Security Council, the leftist government of Guatemala appealed in June, 1954, to the Council as well as to the Organization of American States, alleging the existence of a threat to the peace through aggression by forces gathered in the territory of two of its neighbours. At the first meeting of the Council on the subject, held dramatically on a Sunday (one delegate attended in sports clothes), the item was inscribed on the agenda and debate then deferred so that the Organization of American States, a regional organization, could deal with the matter. That Organization, of course, was bound to inform the Council of the outcome of its action. A week later, the Guatemalan government, obviously in difficulties, again brought the matter before the Council. On this occasion the

United States opposed even inscription. I had the unpleasant task of speaking against the United States' attitude and was supported by Lebanon, Denmark, and the Soviet Union. The Soviet, of course, was merely trying to help a pro-Communist government in Guatemala. But Lebanon, Denmark, and New Zealand were fighting for the principle that every government, great or small, irrespective of its politics, had a right to be heard in the Council. After the Guatemalan government had been heard, the Council once again could have referred the matter to the Organization of American States, and the jurisdiction of a regional organization would have been safeguarded. The United States secured a narrow majority against inscription, with Britain and France abstaining from voting.

New Zealand agreed with the majority that the regional organization was best equipped to investigate and, if possible, to deal with the complaint. However, we felt obliged—and here we differed with some members of the Council, including the United States—to uphold the right of any member of the United Nations to a hearing by the Council on an alleged threat to peace. The particular circumstances of this case, we felt, demanded that the Council should, as a minimum, maintain the question on its agenda until the Organization of American States had completed an investigation and reported to the Security Council.

The Council's jurisdiction, in short, should not be limited by the initiation of concurrent action in a regional organization. At the opening of the twelfth session of the Assembly, I was interested to note the support given this principle in speeches by members of the Organization of American States, including Argentina, Ecuador, and Uruguay. I am well aware that the United States earnestly and sincerely supported a different view, and I appreciate the important political considerations involved. But hard cases make bad law. The principle of the universal and overriding authority of the Security Council is one which to my government seemed well worth maintaining against the happier day when it might be less affected by the strains of Great Power conflicts of interest. While regional organizations are at present an indispensable support to international peace and security they, like the Assembly, cannot fully replace the Security Council.

Of course my government had no sympathy with the Soviet view expressed at the first meeting of the Security Council and the Guatemalan item, which would indicate that the Security Council alone should take immediate steps to end aggression. We fully supported the principle of collective security through regional organizations. This is natural as we are parties to the ANZUS and SEATO treaties. Indeed, both the ANZUS and SEATO treaties recognise the commitment to inform the Security Council immediately of the defence actions taken under their provisions.

In spite of the veto, I have observed a very steady use of the Security Council by member governments. Nonmembers have also resorted to it. Questions so varied as the Guatemalan complaint, Thailand's anxiety over its northern borders, the offshore island crisis, the Hungarian situation, and of course, the great and small problems of the Middle East have come before the Council. Reference to this organ of the United Nations has apprised the world of a crisis and put governments everywhere on their guard. Whenever a threat to peace is involved, resort to the Assembly always may be had under the Uniting for Peace procedure.

That the Council could be made more effective by the

elimination of the veto in certain cases, such as the peaceful settlement of disputes and the admission of new members, goes without saying. But as Russia desires to retain the veto, which cannot be eliminated without her consent or that of all the Great Powers, arguments for improving the Charter in this respect are not very realistic.

During my terms as President of the Council I was able to use the "consensus" procedure. I do not claim to be the originator of this, but I probably relied on it to a greater extent than did any of my predecessors. When I had reason to believe that the Soviet might invoke the veto at the end of the debate, I summed up briefly the views of members and announced what the consensus of opinion was. There was then no voting. Occasionally there was no dissent from the Soviet which might in a given case have no objection to the informality of the consensus procedure. If they wished to record their dissent, they were protected. But the consensus on a given point by most of the members had considerable influence on the parties to a dispute.

The Council is always available, a body specially designed for the solution of problems of peace and war. There is no substitute for it. Admitting all its failures, its defects, and its handicaps, in the last resort its effectiveness depends on the use the nations are prepared to make of it. From my experience the nations of the world are certainly prepared and willing to resort to the Council, in spite of the veto. The responsibility of all members of the Council, and particularly of the Great Power members, is therefore vast: to fulfil in this Council some of the expectations and the hopes of the world.

CHAPTER V

A Declaration
of Human Rights

AT EVERY REGULAR SESSION OF THE ASSEMBLY ITS MEMBERS concern themselves with the question of universal human rights. The debates are long, the resolutions are numerous, and the results are meagre. Unquestionably, human rights are violated over widespread areas. There are concentration camps in Russia and in China. The government of Communist China seeks to impose communism on Tibet with guns, in spite of a promise that the Tibetans would enjoy internal autonomy. In areas apart from Asia, arbitrary arrest, imprisonment without trial, and summary executions still persist.

I recall the Assembly's pronouncement on December 10, 1948, that the Universal Declaration of Human Rights represents "a common standard of achievement for all people and all nations, to the end that every individual and every organ of society, keeping this Declaration constantly in mind, shall strive by *teaching and education* to promote respect for these rights and freedoms and by progressive measures, national and international, to secure their universal and effective recognition and observance, both among the peoples of member states themselves and among the peoples of territories under their jurisdiction."

The formulation of the Declaration was a considerable achievement. To anybody coming from my country the rights set forth in the Declaration would hardly need re-emphasis today. They are taken for granted by us, but not, alas, by some others. As Anglo-Saxons we are concerned more with remedies for the breach of rights. It is all very well to proclaim that no one shall be subjected to arbitrary arrest or detention. But the great question is how can those who are arbitrarily arrested and detained secure their freedom and, in particular, an inquiry by a properly constituted court into the reasons for the detention, followed by release if the reasons prove unsatisfactory. The writ of habeas corpus in English law—that salutary procedure against an unrighteous gaoler—is really of much more significance, in my opinion, than the declaration that every subject shall be free from wrongful arrest.

Nevertheless, I respect the view of Professor Rene Cassin that the idea of drawing up the Universal Declaration was principally born of a desire to protest against the atrocities of the Second World War. Therefore, said the Professor, it has since come to be realised that the document met not only a temporary need of reacting against the violence done to human rights but that it answered a timeless and universal urge.

What is being done to render the Universal Declaration effective? Year after year the Third Committee of the Assembly meets to draft and debate covenants which, when states subscribe to them, will put teeth into the Declaration. Now I agree that we must ceaselessly try to secure observance of the Declaration, although whether covenants can be secured is more than doubtful. There are strong opponents to the notion of covenants; there are equally the pessimists who say that the Declaration will never be transformed into covenants having the effect of treaties. In this, as in other fields, we must not despair. Thus, although the problem of disarmament seems so often insoluble, we never cease to procure a solution. Failure in this field might lead to our destruction.

I believe that we must never abandon our efforts to make the Universal Declaration effective in every part of the world. There still are concentration camps, and places where human beings are coerced and herded as if they were insensate mobs. In a sense the problem of the protection of human rights is more clamant than that of disarmament because millions of human beings at this very moment are being denied their elementary rights.

In the words of General George C. Marshall to the Assembly in 1948, "Governments which systematically disregard the rights of their own people are not likely to respect the rights of other nations and other people and are likely to seek their objectives by coercion and force in the international field."

I trust that I shall not be accused of being a pessimist if I mention some of the difficulties Moses Moskowitz, in his able book, *Human Rights and World Order*, refers to the legal technicalities which occupy the reverent attention of the jurist "as he surveys the Articles of the Charter dealing with the objectives of promoting respect for, and observance of, human rights and fundamental freedoms for all." But I feel that some of the difficulties go far beyond legal technicalities and to the root of the policies of governments and to assertions of sovereignty and of domestic jurisdiction. Most states are peculiarly tender concerning these matters.

In her comprehensive *History of the Charter*, Ruth Russell analyses the problem. We start with the premise that without effective sanctions, a bill of rights cannot be made binding on all states. What are the sanctions to be? If the courts, we shall say, of Hungary, do not protect the individual in his personal rights, the absence of a domestic remedy would logically lead to the idea of an appeal to an international tribunal. Would Hungary, which is a member of the United Nations, have ever dreamt of giving the leader of the Hungarian Revolution, the unfortunate Imre Nagy, the right of appeal to such a tribunal? Unfortunately the question has only to be posed to be answered. Miss Russell has observed that it would be against all previous experience for states to accept the jurisdiction of an international court over their citizens as individuals, particularly in matters relating to their protection by the very government that was being charged with a violation of the bill of rights.

Let us pass beyond individuals to the rights of a minority, rights which were so shockingly swept aside in Nazi Germany. The League proved powerless to deal with the problem. Nor did the democracies do much about it, although they did succour and harbour refugees. A state may in the formulation of its national policy and out of fear, well founded or not, decide to place some restrictions on the freedom of movements of a minority. Should this be a matter for ultimate reference to a world tribunal or to an Assembly with vastly greater power than the present Assembly of the United Nations? We might all have some difficulty in answering that question.

Normally, the present Assembly of the United Nations has no legislative powers. When human rights were violated in Hungary in 1956—and they continue to be violated—all that the Assembly could do was to pass resolutions condemning the Hungarian government and deploring the Soviet Union's massive and bloody intervention. It was powerless to do more. Its member governments were not themselves prepared to introduce sanctions which might have led to a Third World War.

As Mr. Moskowitz regretfully declares, "the United Nations cannot by international action, in its own right, ensue observance of human rights and fundamental freedoms." But it can, I think, express the moral disapprobation of the free world and in the long run we can hope that this will lead to better standards in the totalitarian countries. To abandon this hope is to abandon hope for a better world. Thus I am unwilling to believe that the class of technicians now of such importance in Russia, as a class which will grow, will always tolerate the type of repression which forced Pasternak to decline the Nobel Peace Prize.

No more controversial issue exists in the United Nations than the one of domestic jurisdiction. For these who claim exclusive jurisdiction over the affairs within their own country, however controversial and embittered these may be, however much they involve the suppression of a minority or a majority by those of another race, then the famous terms of Article 2(7) of the Charter are their sword and buckler.

Article 2(7) provides:

Nothing contained in the present Charter shall authorize the United Nations to intervene in matters which are essentially within the domestic jurisdiction of any state or shall require the members to submit such matters to settlement under the present Charter.

If there is a danger of a war, that is another matter. But the supporters of a strict interpretation of this Article are in a minority in the Assembly and even that minority is decreasing. Nevertheless the majority cannot enforce their views. How do the majority argue? They support the view of Judge Sir Hersch Lauterpacht, now the United Kingdom member of the International Court of Justice, that the rule that a state can treat its subjects according to discretion is dependent upon its international obligations—"in particular the general obligations of the Charter of the United Nations relating to human rights and freedoms."

Even those members chary of voting for resolutions calling upon a member government to alter its internal policies feel that the Charter is not infringed by a discussion of the subject in the Assembly or in one of its committees. In other words the argument is that discussion is not tantamount to intervention. Unfortunately intervention is not defined in the Charter. I am rather uneasy about hortatory resolutions urging a particular government to mend its ways. Some of the governments which vote for such resolutions flagrantly ignore, nay, trample upon human rights. Changes must come from *within* a state as a result of the influence of world public opinion and the passage of time. The passage of time *does* work changes in the attitude of governments and of peoples.

There is some evidence that in the early days of the Hungarian revolt in 1956 Russian soldiers were shocked by the repressive measures used and that Russians in Russia itself, particularly students, were stirred in their consciences by the sight of the truckloads of the rebels passing through their country and by the knowledge they gained of the course of events in Hungary. Not even dictators can permanently repress such feelings which are inherent in all human beings except the most callous and ruthless followers of a doctrine.

The payment of compensation to Israel with respect to Nazi confiscations by the government of Western Germany is evidence of how governments change and recognise their responsibility for the acts of their predecessor in violation of human rights.

Can human rights be adequately asserted and protected if an aggrieved citizen of a state cannot petition to some duly constituted international body? I shall not labour this controversial subject. There are those who follow the traditional assumption—that international law is for states and between states and not for the individual to invoke. Certainly this is the Soviet view, and it has many other adherents.

In my judgment the course of the modern development of international law shows, in the words of Moskowitz, a "crumbling of the old doctrine that international law is a system which concerns states alone." This is certainly seen in the provisions of the Charter giving a right of petition to the inhabitants of trusteeship territories. They can petition either the Trusteeship Council or the Fourth Committee. Either body can hear them in person, and petitions may be transmitted directly to the Secretary-General without the intervention of the administering authority. As a former President of the Trusteeship Council it has been my pleasure to hear petitioners from Africa and the Pacific, clad so picturesquely, earnestly expressing their views to the Council.

This procedure has come to stay. It gives rise to administrative burdens and difficulties. The petitions have become numerous, and often the subject matter is not appropriate for the United Nations. Frequently the petitioner has not exhausted the remedies available to him in the trusteeship territory or it is obvious he is a person with an unjustified sense of grievance. It may well be that a body should be established to eliminate at an early stage petitions which are obviously unworthy of the attention of the Trusteeship Council. But the Soviet jealously upholds an unrestricted right of petition in the Trusteeship Council and the Fourth Committee, where it seeks to embarrass the so-called colonial powers.

I can understand the attitude of those who consider that human rights, to be effective, will have to be safeguarded by a right of petition to some international body, available to individuals but with safeguards administrative and legal. Undoubtedly there would have to be a preliminary sifting of petitions.

It has been further suggested by the Uruguayan Delegation that the United Nations should appoint an Attorney-General, who would receive complaints from individuals or groups alleging breaches of the suggested covenant of human rights. He would undertake their preliminary examination and investigation and seek a satisfactory settlement by negotiation with the party concerned. Where sufficient ground for doing so existed, the Attorney-General would present the case before a Human Rights Committee for examination and determination of the substance of the complaint. The Attorney-General would be there to plead impartially the case of the international community. The theory, at any rate, of his appointment and function is that he would forestall the intervention of a foreign government in a dispute between a citizen and his own government. I think this assumption of doubtful validity.

Such are the proposals. No covenant has yet been entered

into and therefore no Human Rights Committee pursuant to it has been established, and the draft covenant which, if it were adopted, would establish such a committee, expressly provides that an aggrieved person cannot invoke its provisions without the intervention of a foreign government. In other words, the framers of the draft covenant follow the doctrine of international law that that law is for states and that individuals can derive their rights only through states. We may deplore this, but it is the attitude adopted by most members of the United Nations.

In the present state of international opinion I think there is little chance of such an Attorney-General being appointed with the powers suggested. Moreover, if an individual is given the right to appeal to an international body like the suggested Committee for Human Rights, I do not yet see how to prevent, under such circumstances, a dissident and rebellious minority from abusing the right to petition and thereby subverting the lawful authority of its state.

This brings me back to my feeling that it is only from within itself that a defaulting state will learn to respect human rights. I confess sympathy with the views of the late John Foster Dulles that it is by methods of persuasion, education, and example that all states will advance to the observance of human rights rather than by treaties and covenants "which would commit one part of the world to impose its particular social and moral standards upon another part of the world community, which has different standards."

CHAPTER VI

One Court for the World

Now, we are seeking to establish world order based on the assumption that the collective life of nations ought to be governed by law—as formulated in the Charter of the United Nations and other international treaties, and law as enunciated in international courts. . . .

To accomplish peace through law will take patience and perseverance. It will require us at times to provide an example by accepting for ourselves standards of conduct more advanced than those generally accepted.

—John Foster Dulles at the New York State Bar Association, January 31, 1959

As a step toward creating the rule of law among nations, the charter established the International Court of Justice, which essentially is the same as the Permanent Court of International Justice that functioned under the League.

The judicial branch of the United Nations is generally regarded as its weakest limb. Composed of fifteen eminent jurists sitting in great dignity at The Hague, far removed from the tumult and the pressures of New York, the Court by April, 1959, had disposed of an average of only two cases a year. Some nations have flouted its opinions. One has refused to pay the compensation the Court directed it to pay. Some states are reluctant to resort to the Court when they are aware in advance that the majority of its members are opposed to their policies and legal approach.

The Charter itself deals briefly with the Court. Each member undertakes to comply with a decision in any case to which it is a party. What if a member fails to discharge this obligation? At first sight the relevant provision of the Charter looks convincing. The aggrieved party "may have recourse to the Security Council, which may, if it deems necessary, make recommendations or decide upon measures to be taken to give effect to the judgment."

No state has availed itself of this provision. The Security Council has a discretion to intervene, but it would not intervene unless a threat to the peace were involved, and the veto could stultify it.

The Charter provides that the Assembly or the Security Council may request the Court to give an advisory opinion on any legal question. But such opinion means what it says: it is advisory and is not binding. Nevertheless, the Court's advisory opinions have been of great value in the development of international law.

These provisions of the Charter are not exhaustive. Attached to the Charter and forming part of it is the Statute of the Court. Its provisions are important, because the Court, as the principal judicial organ of the United Nations, is obligated to function in accordance with the Statute.

The Statute's first provision of importance prescribes the method of electing the fifteen judges who hold office for nine years, may be re-elected, receive a handsome emolument free of tax, and enjoy diplomatic privileges and immunities. Continuity of membership is ensured by elections being held at three-year intervals, five seats being filled at a time.

Naturally those chosen must be independent; they must not engage in any political or administrative function or in any profession. In the Court as a whole the representation of the main forms of civilisation and of the principal legal systems of the world should be assured. Thus the Court has Communist judges and, at one time or another, judges from most nations of the world except Communist China.

The influence of the French concept of law and of judicial functions is strong in the Court. Some of its judgments are often overcompendious, and when collective do not embody the sustained reasoning characteristic of British and American judicial opinions. Where dissent occurs, a detailed, dissenting judgment by an experienced judge is of value and the Court's influence would be enhanced by more of such opinions.

A judge must be elected by an absolute majority in both the Assembly and the Security Council. There is no veto in the latter, probably because in the earlier days of the formation of the Charter the Russians were not so obsessed by the veto.

Candidates are nominated by national groups which consult their highest courts of justice, law schools, and academies devoted to the study of law. No state may have more than one judge, but this does not preclude the British Commonwealth's having judges elected from each of its members. Thus in the present Court are a judge from the United Kingdom, from Australia, and from Pakistan. Sir Mulhammad Zafrulla Khan of Pakistan, a great Moslem judge, was formerly of the Federal Court of India and has a profound knowledge of the English common law and the Moslem and Hindu systems of law.

Provision is made for *ad hoc* judges where the Court includes no judge of the nationality of the parties. Lobbying for election is generally intense. The government of a candidate approaches all other governments where there is a possibility of a disputed election. Delegates are lobbied in the Assembly Hall and the lounges. Many a candidate approaches his friends, and pressures are considerable. Recently when a Chinese judge died, the State Department canvassed successfully to have his post filled by Dr. Wellington Koo, the former Chinese Ambassador to Washington. The contest between Sir Zafrulla Khan and an Indian nominee was equally vigorous.

The influence of the Security Council is predominant. Providing its members remain firm, the majority for another candidate in the Assembly gradually whittles away. As President during the election of judges, I have announced that there was no absolute majority for a particular jurist in either organ and I am afraid that I have watched with rather cynical detachment as the Security Council eventually had its way.

All this raises the question whether the judges ever act from political motives. Long ago Mr. Dooley said that the Supreme Court of the United States reads the election returns. There have been allegations that judges on both the Permanent Court and the present Court have been influenced by political considerations.

On the whole, I think that the Court emerges well from these criticisms. Professor Oliver J. Lissitzyn, in his United Nations study of the Court, writes:

> . . . It is generally true that the various members of the Court and especially judges *ad hoc* "have usually supported the

contentions of the governments of which they were nationals
or by which they were appointed," although there have been
numerous exceptions. It must be remembered, moreover, that
direct national interest in the outcome of a particular case is
not the only possible cause of partiality. No member of the
Court has even been accused of being swayed by considerations of personal gain, but sympathy for a particular group
of states or their political and social institutions may have
influenced some judges. Furthermore, it is not improbable
that some judges have been inclined to favour the historical
positions or interest of their own states even in cases in which
these states were not parties.

A notable case of a judge dissenting from the views of his
own government was the opinion of the present Lord McNair
in the case arising out of the seizure by the Iranian government of the Anglo-Iranian Oil Company's wells and refinery.

Professor Lissitzyn concludes that it would be unrealistic
to deny that there has been some bias out of the clashes of
policy between the Soviet bloc and the Western nations. Yet
we should remember that in interpreting Federal constitu-
tions, eminent and irreproachable judges in a state itself are
consciously or unconsciously influenced by social and economic trends in their country.

International law is incomplete and uncertain in many
matters. It has been proposed that it should be codified, but
national experience proves that codification is never a complete enunciation of any branch of the law. Judges will develop it by filling in blanks and by removing uncertainties;
through their interpretation they will adapt a code to new
circumstances. If this is true of codification within a state, it
will be realised how difficult is the work of the International
Court where uncertainties and gaps in the law are so great

and there is no codification. The Court will still be impartial if it gives precedence to its "own conceptions of what the long-range interests of the international community require over the interests of the particular parties to a dispute."

A notable case of the Court laying down its conception of these requirements is when it gave an advisory opinion on the right of the United Nations to obtain reparation for the deaths and injuries of its agents in Palestine, in particular the assassination of Count Bernadotte. The Court held that the United Nations had an international personality and therefore the capacity to present international claims. Israel accepted the Court's opinion. But I incline to the view that the Court went too far in saying that the long-range policy of the international community, as shaped in the United Nations by the dominant group of its members, should prevail, at least to some extent, over particular states who opposed their international positions being modified without their consent. This would be to give the United Nations a supraworld power which it does not possess.

It is when we come to the question of the extent of the Court's jurisdiction that we see the limitations of its powers. Only a certain number of states have agreed that the Court should have compulsory jurisdiction. This extends to such matters as the interpretation of a treaty, any question of international law, the existence of any fact which, if established, would constitute the breach of international obligation and the nature or extent of the compensation for such a breach. Neither the Soviet Union nor the United States has accepted the compulsory jurisdiction of the Court.

Since the Soviet Union represents what it calls a socialistic society, its attitude may be expressed simply. As the majority

of the judges on the Court are, in the Soviet view, representatives of capitalistic states, the Communist judges will
be outvoted. Therefore, the Soviet Union refuses to accept
in advance the judgments of the Court.

The reason for the attitude of the United States is entirely
different. The United States negotiators for the establishment
of the International Court feared that if the Administration
agreed to compulsory jurisdiction, the Senate would refuse
to adopt the Charter, or at any rate adhere to the Court.
Moreover there was the consideration that to accept the compulsory jurisdiction of the Court might impinge on State
rights in the United States. Consequently, the United States
did not accept the jurisdiction of the Court until 1946, when
it resolved that the Court's jurisdiction would not apply "to
matters which are essentially within the domestic jurisdiction
of the United States." This was reasonable enough but the
acceptance of jurisdiction was qualified by the so-called Connally Amendment, which provided that the United States
would itself determine what were domestic disputes and
therefore not within the Court's jurisdiction. Other countries
have adopted this amendment. I agree with Senator Hum-
phrey: as a result the Court has operated with its hands tied.

In a speech delivered on April 13, 1959, Vice-President
Richard M. Nixon said that the Administration would submit
shortly to the recommendations by Congress to modify the
Connally Amendment. I profoundly hope that this will be
achieved; otherwise, in many cases the Court will continue
to be ineffective.

A further example of a limitation in the Court's jurisdiction
is a declaration made by the United Kingdom on April 18,
1957, excluding from the Court's decision "any question

which in the opinion of the government of the United Kingdom affects the national security of the United Kingdom or any of its dependent territories."

In the present state of its development, the Court is not a suitable tribune for dealing with questions involving the enforcement of peace. A judicial body is not adapted to dealing with political matters. One former United Nations official, Ahmed Bokhari, went so far as to say that major disputes still tend to be regarded as political situations amenable to political remedies rather than legal situations which need to be submitted to judicial scrutiny. Neither the Court nor the United Nations has a permanent police force at its disposal. In every country the courts know that in the last resort the police normally will enforce their decisions. I say "normally" because even a Court of a state delivering a judgment having political implications may find difficulties in its enforcement. I agree with Professor Lissitzyn that no international police force can succeed in enforcing peace until it is backed by a strong sense of the imperative character of world law. This is difficult to achieve when sovereignty and nationalism are so potent and international law is so uncertain.

In his valuable book *The Common Law of Mankind*, Wilfred Jenks writes with cogency:

> The disruptive effects of the Second World War and the cold war; the challenge which they represent to the basic concepts of a family of nations, the rule of law, and the overriding claims of common humanity; the striking manner in which they have destroyed, apparently permanently, the balance of power among a group of States sharing a common civilisation and common conceptions of morality which—however rightly we may, during the period immediately following the

First World War, have criticised its limitations as a device for maintaining the peace in the absence of an effective international organisation—was nevertheless one of the essential foundations of the community of international law; the scale on which and speed at which they have released and given opportunities of decisive influence to new political forces which have not yet learned from the facts of international life the habit of respect for international law; and the extent to which they have created or intensified economic and social problems for which international law is still in process of finding appropriate solutions: all these factors have tended to produce a situation of grave uncertainty which has given rise to widespread and deeply rooted pessimism.

Nevertheless I am not pessimistic. I recall reading what little work the Supreme Court in the United States was called upon to do in its early years. Gradually it obtained its present distinguished position and produced a great body of decisions dealing with the constitutional relations between the Republic and member states. As the world community slowly develops, the International Court will deliver more and more decisions defining legal relations between states and between the United Nations and states.

We should remember that only after many centuries of effort and suffering do we now maintain the rule of law in the modern democratic state with the help of its enlightened public opinion, a legislature capable of appreciating and meeting the need for change, courts whose decisions are enforced and, last but not least, a police force. Lawyers speak of the "seamless web of law." The International Court in its development of international law is slowly weaving the web of international law.

Already it has delivered some important decisions, no less

significant because they have been few in number. Thus, in the Corfu Channel case, a distinguished member of the Court, Judge H. Lauterpacht, has pointed out that the judgment is not only a contribution to the question of the position of international straits and the meaning of innocent passage, it is an authority, directly or indirectly, on other matters: the right of intervention and self-help; the interpretation of treaties, especially of those conferring jurisdiction upon the Court; the responsibility of states for injury done within their territory to other states; the damages for breach of an international duty; and the evidence in international proceedings. Unfortunately in this case Albania has refused to pay the damages awarded to the United Kingdom.

It is encouraging to remember that Mr. Dulles, in speaking to the New York Bar Association, said that the Administration was closely examining the question of the United States relationship to the Court with a view to see whether ways and means could be found to assure a greater use of the Court by the United States and through its example by others. The International Court can grow in stature and influence only as the greatest power in the free world makes increasing use of it and seeks always to strengthen its membership.

CHAPTER VII

Trusteeship Council: Adviser and Protector

THE GENERAL PUBLIC IS LESS FAMILIAR WITH THE TRUSTEESHIP Council, the supervisory body of the multifarious trusteeship territories, than with all the other organs of the United Nations. This is unfortunate because the objectives of the trusteeship system are far-reaching, and it affects the destiny of millions in Africa and in the Pacific.

The governments of the West are painfully aware that there is a struggle for men's minds in the strategic continent of Africa with its vast resources and backward peoples and that the outcome of this struggle will affect the balance of power in the world. The work of the Trusteeship Council has a decisive bearing on the outcome.

The Charter defines the basic objectives of the trusteeship system as the furthering of international peace and security and the promotion of the political, economic, racial, and educational development of the trust territories. Then we come to the nub of the matter. The prime objective, certainly the one which appeals above all to the anticolonial powers, is the "progressive development of the trusteeship territories toward self-government or independence as may be appropriate to the particular circumstances of each territory and its peoples and the freely expressed wishes of the peoples concerned and as may be provided by the terms of each trusteeship agreement."

Note that self-government and independence are distinguished, although independence appears as the sole objective to the Russians in the Trusteeship Council. Further, regard is to be had to the appropriate circumstances of each territory. When hearing the Soviet representative, often one would think that the policy of his government was to urge independence for Tanganyika almost as soon as the target date for self-government fixed for the comparatively advanced territory of Western Samoa.

The other objectives of the system are the encouragement of respect for human rights and fundamental freedoms and the recognition of the interdependence of the peoples of the world. Finally, the system is designed to ensure equal treatment in trusteeship territories in social, economic, commercial, and legal matters for all members of the United Nations and their nationals. This provision is subject to treaties existing before 1945 which may have given a state special rights, for example, in trade with a trusteeship territory.

How does the system work? A state administering a trusteeship territory has entered into an agreement with the United Nations which set the terms. The Charter authorises one or more states of the organization itself to administer. The only example of more than one state constituting an authority is the trusteeship of the phosphate-producing island of Nauru in the central Pacific, where Australia, New Zealand, and the United Kingdom are designated as the administering authorities but in fact Australia acts for the three. And incidentally, as an example of the complexity of the trusteeship system, when the phosphates are worked out in roughly forty years, another island will have to be found for the Nauruans who number only some 2,000.

There is no example of the organization itself acting as a trustee, although a special international regime for Jerusalem was proposed in the Trusteeship Council, but never came to pass. The Charter does not describe the machinery for an international trusteeship. Undoubtedly it would be cumbersome. But today there are proposals for an international trusteeship of Antarctica; as it has no indigenous inhabitants, the legal basis for a trusteeship appears to be wanting.

The membership of the Council is equally divided between administering and nonadministering authorities. This often gives rise to conflicting political considerations, with the Soviet Union consistently wielding the anticolonial stick and posing as friend, guide, and mentor to the African peoples aspiring to independence.

The Council is a very different body from the Permanent Mandates Commission, its predecessor under the League. The Council sits in public; the Commission sat in private. The Council has many political appointees, although some of its representatives are and have been distinguished colonial administrators; the Commission "was a semi-judicial body whose members were selected for their outstanding personal qualifications and their independence of governments." The Council sends regular visiting missions to the various trusteeship territories; the Commission had no such power.

The Commission inquired into the administration of the mandated territories. These territories, with the exception of German Southwest Africa, became trusteeship territories after

1945. The International Court of Justice, in an advisory opinion, has held that the Union of South Africa continues to have international obligations under the mandate, that the United Nations is entitled to exercise supervisory functions over the administration of the mandate, and that the Union acting alone is not competent to modify the international status of the territory. The Union has declined to accept this and subsequent advisory opinions. This vexed question continues to trouble the Assembly, while the Union virtually incorporates the area in its territory.

The Trusteeship Council, even though it exercises no jurisdiction over former German Southwest territory, has more than enough to keep its members fully occupied. Since 1945 it has inquired in detail every year into the affairs of Tanganyika, Ruanda-Urundi, the Cameroons and Togoland under British and French administration, New Guinea, Nauru, the northern Pacific islands under United States administration, Italian Somaliland, and Western Samoa. The work of the Council involves studying and debating voluminous reports from the administering authorities or from visiting missions, hearing petitioners, setting up committees to draft recommendations which it debates and settles, nominating and dispatching visiting missions to far-flung trusteeship territories, and presenting an annual report to the Assembly.

The inhabitants of the trust territories may rest assured that the Council protects their interests and scrutinises their grievances. Almost invariably an expert, called a special representative from the trust territory and appointed by the administrating authority, is present at the appropriate Council meeting to give a comprehensive statement and to answer the most searching questions.

Much of the work of the Trusteeship Council tends to be duplicated on the Fourth Committee which for many days debates the Council's annual report, frequently pre-hears petitioners, and passes draft resolutions that come before the Assembly for debate and vote. In dealing with some of these resolutions, the Assembly exercises legislative or quasi-legislative powers, particularly when with the consent of the Administering Authority it adopts resolutions for the attainment of self-government and the end of a trusteeship.

To evaluate the work of the Trusteeship Council, one must have some knowledge of the events leading to its creation and of the policy of the United States, the United Kingdom, and the Soviet Union toward dependent territories. One must also remember that India, an important member of the Council only recently and not long an independent state, has many officials who are experts in the art of territorial administration and who were trained under the British.

In her *History of the United Nations Charter,* Miss Ruth B. Russell writes:

Although the United States had rejected Woodrow Wilson's ideas on international organization after the First World War, Americans widely approved his concept of self-determination and in the course of time extended its application to all colonial peoples. American views on this question, colored by recollections of the colonial origins of the United States, have been prone to a basic oversimplification that, in essence, assumed that "colonialism" and "imperialism" were bad by nature, that "freedom" and "self-determination" were synonymous and that no people, therefore, should be denied the right to independence. Government officials shared this view with members of Congress and the public at large. Before the Second World War, this predilection was reinforced by the action of the United States Government itself in 1936, when it guaranteed the Philippines their independence after a specified time.

The United States leaders and officials had to proceed carefully in enunciating their views which far from met the approval of Mr. Churchill. He announced firmly that he had not "become the King's First Minister in order to preside over the liquidation of the British Empire." The United States' views themselves underwent some modification when the Departments of War and of Navy urged the postwar control of bases in the northern Pacific for security purposes. In fact, there are numerous islands in the northern Pacific which are subject to what is called strategic trusteeship by the United States. The United States reports on its administration of these islands to the Trusteeship Council, which in turn adopts the report that it transmits to the Security Council. The United States has held itself free to conduct nuclear explosions within these islands, although not without criticism from some members of the Council. The Council has declined to refer the question of the legality of these tests to the International Court for an advisory opinion.

Of particular importance is the American support of the fixing of a target date for the establishment of independence in trusteeship territories. The United States has observed its own target date in giving the Philippines their independence and cites this as an example to other countries. I do not think, however, that in the stage of the government of certain trusteeship territories a target date is possible or wise. This seems to me to be particularly true in the cases of Tanganyika, Ruanda-Urundi, New Guinea, and Nauru. Conditions in New Guinea are most primitive, and only now are its inhabitants emerging from savagery. Recently frequent fighting and raids developed between tribes in remote areas.

The consistent aim of the United Kingdom has been to advance the inhabitants of dependent territories toward self-government or independence. Mr. Churchill's famous statement did not involve any interruption of this policy, which in India was realised by the Labor Government that succeeded him. But I think I might properly say that British governments do not believe in precipitate haste and appreciate the necessity to equip the peoples of trusteeship territories with techniques in politics, health, economics, and education so that they may achieve and preserve genuine self-government or independence.

The Soviet Union, of course, takes an entirely different line, in spite of the fact that it has seized power in many ancient states in Eastern Europe. Its attitude may be gauged by the Soviet representative's comment at the Council's Twenty-second Session dealing with the territory of New Guinea. The Soviet representative said:

> . . . that the situation in this Trust Territory showed that the indigenous inhabitants occupied a secondary place in the mind of the Administering Authority, and the measures it took were designed to consolidate the domination of a small minority representing the interests of the Administering Authority itself. In this connexion the United Nations should receive indubitable and convincing evidence of the fact that the end purpose of the Trusteeship System, independence or self-government, would not turn into a mirage for the indigenous population. One of these proofs should be the setting of a time-table for the achievement of independence. Whatever the irritation shown by the Administering Authority towards the decisions of the General Assembly, it was the

duty of the Council to remind the Administering Authority that it had not carried out the resolution of the General Assembly on this important issue.

It is astounding that a Soviet spokesman, well aware of his country's iron rule in the satellites, should dare to suggest the setting of a time-table for independence for New Guinea, where the Australians after enormous difficulties are endeavouring to promote the well-being of some of the most primitive peoples of the world. Indeed, the Council at the Twenty-second Session noted that the Australian government considered it impractical to fix rigid dates.

However, early in the history of the United Nations a target date was fixed for the independence of Somaliland in 1960. Many feel that this date is premature; but the United Nations is committed to it. It is recognised that the known economic resources of this territory are meagre, and that most of the inhabitants lead a basically self-sufficient nomadic or semi-nomadic existence. The budget operates on a considerable deficit. Who will make up this deficit when independence is achieved nobody knows, although some members of the Council hopefully urge that the Italians should assist in this direction. Probably the cost will fall on the United Nations, in other words, on member states, and therefore the United States will be the chief benefactor. The Italian government has done excellent work in preparing this extremely poor territory as best it can for independence.

Soon Western Samoa, which is under New Zealand's administration, will achieve self-government or independence. Often in the Council the New Zealand administration has been praised as a model. Even so, Western Samoa is a small area with only some 97,000 people who would find independence in the modern world a matter of some difficulty. They are likely to depend on New Zealand for the conduct of defence and foreign affairs.

It is a matter of inspiration to watch the development under the Trusteeship System of people like the Western Samoans and the Africans in the Cameroons and Togoland. Indeed British Togoland is now part of the free state of Ghana. A note of caution: today there is a tendency toward what I call fragmentation of sovereignty. Small and new states in the modern world, lacking modern techniques, are a lure to the predatory. Admiring, as I do in general, the work of the Trusteeship Council, I am an apostle of gradualism. I have heard Krishna Menon, however, say that better bad self-government than government by another state. He and his delegation have played a most valuable part in assisting in the Council's deliberations affecting the trusteeship territories, but I hope that he will realise that premature self-government in a territory like Tanganyika is not conducive to the stability of that territory or its neighbours and would indeed affect the progress of Africa as a whole.

CHAPTER VIII

Policy Making in the Delegates' Lounge

Dulce est desipere in loco.

—Horace

It is pleasant to relax in the delegates' lounge.

—Almost any delegate

YOU MAY KNOW A POLITICAL PARTY BY ITS PLACES OF EASE AND relaxation as well as by its formal halls. This is certainly true of the Assembly and of the Delegates' Lounge. Through the Lounge's great glass windows delegates may look out on lawns and gardens, the equestrian statue of a hero of Yugoslavia (who never thought of communism), a skyline of hotels and apartments, and the swift-flowing East River. Those who stand at the bar, where many gather before lunch and in the evening, may turn and gaze on one of the loveliest views in New York, whether in summer or in winter, past Welfare Island toward the great bridges spanning the blue river and its boats and barges. It is in this Lounge that the President and the Secretary-General receive kings and queens and presidents. Here, after her speech in the Assembly, Queen Elizabeth II and Prince Philip met many delegates.

At about quarter to one when the Assembly and the committees adjourn, most of the delegates and their staffs walk toward the Lounge, save a few foreign ministers and others whose high duties summon them elsewhere or who find it unhelpful to confront the Press or mingle with the lesser ranks of the diplomatic world. At this time in the Lounge and at the height of the Assembly there is scarcely room to move. A Spaniard is jostled by a Sudanese; British, Australians, and New Zealanders gather with Indians, Pakistans, and Malayans; a few women from Europe sit smoking cheroots; and journalists weave their way through them all. There are almost as many guests as delegates, all eager to see celebrities, like the charming and able Prince Aly Khan, an urbane example of Moslem and European civilisation.

The proceedings of the morning are discussed, plans for the afternoon are made, and gossip is exchanged. But among all responsible delegations there is serious preparation for the day and the morrow. I know no staffs more devoted to their tasks and more skilled in performing them than those of the many responsible missions to the United Nations.

Not all delegates or their staffs care to listen throughout the speeches, whether in the Assembly or its committees. Many speeches are long, but time to live and to work is short. Usually only one member of the United States delegation, and one of low rank at that, stays to listen to the long-winded and repetitious speech of a satellite. Some delegates may use the Lounge as an office; most conduct consultations there. Since there is a vast amount of lobbying for votes, whether in the Assembly or the committees, the Lounge becomes an important place.

The delegations of the United States and the United Kingdom invariably appoint for each session of the Assembly a Spanish-speaking diplomat whose task it is to canvass on critical issues the twenty votes of the Latin Americans. Since the entry of the new African and Asian members, the Latin American votes are not so decisive but they are still of great importance and on many occasions may be relied on in support of the West.

I would not suggest that these Latin American votes are easily won. States like Mexico, Brazil, Colombia, Peru, and Argentina are of particular influence. Because Brazil and Colombia have contributed forces both in Korea and in the Middle East, they regard themselves as entitled to an influential voice; Brazil, whose Foreign Office is skilful and experienced, has great weight in the election of a Latin American state to the Security Council. The Chairman of the Latin American bloc for the year will generally sit as his country's representative as a Vice-President of the Assembly. No one can fail to be influenced by the erudition of many Latin American delegates. Mr. Belaunde of Peru is a shining example of learning and humour.

At the end of 1955 the Assembly reached a deadlock concerning the election to one seat on the Security Council. Neither the Philippines nor Yugoslavia could secure the necessary majority. Finally in desperation the President was persuaded to draw lots, a most unorthodox procedure. The President chose to inform the Assembly of what he had done. Had he left the matter to the imagination of the Assembly all might have been well, but the publication of the procedure was too much for some delegates. All of which prompted Mr. Belaunde to say that the Assembly was like a lady who could tolerate a good many things in private but resented their being made public.

Mexico usually pursues a middle course; her vote on any particular subject is not easily obtained. In Dr. Padillo Nervo, a distinguished former Foreign Minister of his country, she has provided a President of the Assembly. The Mexicans take great interest in disarmament and invariably try to influence the Great Powers, but with scant success in view of the intransigence of Russia.

So in the Lounge the great and the small try to influence each other. Normally delegates cannot pledge their countries and have to secure instructions from their capital, but the advice of a delegate is often accepted by his government. "Vote-swapping" is only too frequent. This if "you" will vote for my candidate as chairman of a committee, "I" will vote for you on an issue affecting your government. Sometimes precious little consideration is given to the merits.

The Lounge is an all-important place for ascertaining what governments are doing and particularly what the Great Powers are planning. As is not surprising, they are not always very forthcoming in the earlier stages of policy making. But as the representatives of the small powers often are asked very late in the day to pledge a vote, they constantly seek information so that their governments may be informed in advance of events. The small powers do not like to be used as mere vote-givers. Diplomats, old and young, press around a delegate from the United States or the United Kingdom to ascertain his country's policy. The effort may not always be successful and much time is spent collating scraps of news for a telegram to one's capital.

Various groups consult regularly, especially the Western

Europeans, the Afro-Asians, the Latin Americans, and the Commonwealth. The Americans make a practice of briefing the Latin Americans, in which they are helped by the charm of Henry Cabot Lodge and his ability to speak Spanish. The Russians are close to many of the Afro-Asians. Krishna Menon generally knows the Russian point of view and seeks to be a bridge between the West and the Communists. The Indian government is as well an energetic champion of Communist China's pretensions to the Chinese seat.

No group is of greater importance than the Commonwealth, comprising the United Kingdom, Canada, Australia, the Union of South Africa, New Zealand, India, Pakistan, Ceylon, Malaya, and Ghana, whose peoples total 600,000,000. The delegates of all these countries meet at the United Nations during the session of the Assembly once a week, and various ones confer informally. They do not always agree but when they do their influence is great. Even when they disagree it is important for each to know the reasons for disagreement; in the process of private debate the margin of disagreement may be diminished. Since they all speak a common language and have a common heritage of Parliamentary institutions and law, their consultations are of great value to themselves and to the United Nations.

Not all the leaders of delegations enter the Lounge. For one thing, the Press is always there seeking information with an assiduity and skill which have to be experienced to be believed. The results of the deliberations of some blocs are known within five minutes. Information from one delegate may be checked by the cautious or embarrassed silence of another.

The foreign secretaries of the United Kingdom, the United States, France, and the Soviet Union rarely enter the Lounge.

I never saw the late John Foster Dulles there. After public debate Henry Cabot Lodge invariably goes to his private offices in the Secretariat buildings. No delegation is supposed to have a private office in these buildings, but it is an open secret that the Americans and the British each possess a suite, a reasonable enough privilege considering the extent of their preoccupations and responsibilities.

The Russians do enter the Lounge and since the death of Stalin, a few of them and the satellites patronise the bar, although sparingly. But Andrei Gromyko does not appear. He favours more remote lounges. When the business of the Assembly or a committee is finished, he is generally seen surrounded by a group of his advisers as he walks with rather lugubrious mien to his limousine. The Russians are serious; they work tremendously hard and are assiduous in their attendance at debate. Not for them the blandishments of the coffee break.

Mr. Menon is frequently in the Lounge, not at the bar, for he dislikes liquor, preferring to drink copious cups of tea and to confer with many delegations on the proposals which he launches so constantly and indefatigably, sometimes receiving little welcome in Western Europe. He is skilful in the art of compromise and in the drafting of resolutions. But as one of my predecessors, Sir Carl Berendsen, has said, we need not so many resolutions but resolution in the Assembly. Mr. Menon is at most cocktail parties—and their number is legion —not to drink cocktails but to confer and to plan. His influence with the Afro-Asian group is naturally very great, speaking as he does with the voice of Mr. Nehru, India's Prime Minister.

There are two persons who normally do not enter the Lounge: the President and the Secretary-General.

CHAPTER IX

The President's
Behind-the-Scenes Diplomacy

AFTER I HAD BEEN PRESIDENT OF THE SECURITY COUNCIL AND the Trusteeship Council and Chairman of the First Committee, various member states suggested that I might become President of the Assembly. Many felt that the Commonwealth, which had been represented last by Lester Pearson of Canada in 1952 and 1953, was entitled to have one of its citizens as President of the Twelfth Session in 1957. Madam Pandit, sister of Mr. Nehru, had held office as President in 1953–1954, primarily as the representative of a great Asian country and not of the Commonwealth.

In the result, I was elected President in September, 1957. For some time beforehand, however, it appeared that the election would be contested. Some months after my candidacy had been announced and when already I had received promises of support from many influential governments, including those of the Commonwealth and of all the continents, Dr. Charles Malik, the distinguished representative of Lebanon, entered the field. He worked hard to win.

This was something new in the history of the Presidency. When Madam Pandit had been elected, votes were cast for Prince Wan of Thailand but the contest was not very spirited. My opponent spared no effort and indeed claimed that the stability of the Middle East depended on his success, an argument which I, with others, failed to follow. Dr. Malik secured promises of votes from all the Arab states but, and this is important, in spite of his utmost efforts he could not persuade the great states of India and Pakistan to recede from their promises to me. The United States undertook to support me, as did countries as influential as Mexico, Brazil, Peru, Chile, and the Argentine. Almost all the governments of Western Europe, including France and Italy, were on my side.

Nevertheless, Dr. Malik persisted in his efforts to secure the Presidency until three o'clock on September 17th, when the Assembly met to choose its new head. Shortly before he had asked Prince Wan, the outgoing President, to see if I would withdraw. I remained firm. There was no reason to do otherwise as I had been first in the field and had the support of the large majority of governments, including all the Great Powers, save the Soviet which with its bloc and the Arabs was Dr. Malik's chief source of support.

Prince Wan called the Assembly to order. I was in my seat with the New Zealand delegation. Excitement and uncertainty filled the air. Dr. Padillo Nervo, a former President and then the Foreign Minister of Mexico and a firm supporter of mine, had been in earnest conversation with various delegates. After the opening in silent prayer, Dr. Nervo secured the rostrum, appealing for a unanimous election of the President and the withdrawal of Dr. Malik, who in a moving scene yielded. I was elected with one dissenting vote.

I was duly grateful to my opponent who became my successor in September, 1958, when he himself had to wage a vigorous campaign for the office with Mohammed Mahgoub, the former Foreign Minister of the Sudan. Unlike mine, this election went to vote. It may well be that in the future it will be increasingly difficult to secure unanimity in the election of the President. This is unfortunate because the Assembly's Chief Officer gains in stature and influence when he is a unanimous choice.

By custom the post of President is filled by the representative of a small country, and there is regard for geographical distribution. Europe, the Commonwealth, Latin America, and Asia have provided Presidents, although not yet Africa. After an area has provided a president, normally it will wait its next turn for three to four years. Finally, a candidate for the Presidency is expected to be a citizen of importance in his own country, enjoying the confidence and the support of his government, often its foreign minister at some time, and preferably with experience as chairman of at least one of the committees of the Assembly.

There is nothing in the Charter about the President beyond the provision that the Assembly shall elect its President for each session. The rules of the Assembly provide that the President declare the opening and closing date of a session, that he direct the discussions, rule on points of order and, subject to the rules, have complete control of the proceedings at any meeting and over the maintenance of order.

Mr. Roosevelt, during the drafting of the Charter, contemplated that "as head of the international organization a person of eminent attainment should be elected by the General Assembly, upon nomination by the Executive Council, to serve for a period of three years and not subject to re-election." Such a person of the calibre of a Roosevelt or a

Churchill was to preside over the Executive Council (presumably the Security Council) and at the opening session of the General Assembly, pending the election of its President. He was also to act as adviser to the General Committee. He was to act as Chairman, without vote, of the Security Council. Presumably Mr. Roosevelt anticipated that a person of such eminence would intervene in the Security Council to deal with an impasse produced by the veto. It would be difficult to select a man of the attainments and the experience which Mr. Roosevelt had in mind, acting in such prominent capacities in the Assembly and the Security Council.

In vital matters the Great Powers probably would not tolerate the interference of a President of this type, however eminent. During my term of office the issue of disarmament was hotly debated. Dr. Nervo suggested to some of the Great Powers that I as President should sit as a chairman and in some degree act as a mediator while they met to deal with disarmament. The suggestion met with no enthusiasm. The three Great Powers (the United Kingdom, the United States, and the Soviet Union) have shown that they prefer to deal with certain aspects of disarmament on their own, preferably at Geneva, without the addition of even France or Canada. I am not ignoring the fact that on the Soviet's insistence the Disarmament Commission was enlarged to include the whole Assembly, but this was merely poor window dressing.

When the Great Powers, as in the Suez crisis, delegate certain responsibilities to the Secretary-General rather than to the President, it is because, among other reasons, the Secretary-General has a longer tenure of office and an established position both in the Security Council and in the Assembly.

The Secretary-General can take the initiative in the Security Council where the President of the Assembly has no place. While the Charter does not give an initiative to the Secretary-General in the Assembly, he sits there beside its President and now does not hesitate to take an initiative. In neither place does the Secretary-General have a vote; neither does the President in the Assembly. In the last three years the Secretary-General has grown toward the status which Mr. Roosevelt seems to have had in mind.

That President of Mr. Roosevelt's choice was to be a person of greater significance than the official referred to in the Charter. If the President of the Assembly confined himself to his duties as a chairman he would still be important but not of great political significance. To steer the course of debate, to rule on points of order, to preside over the General Committee, to speak on great ceremonial occasions, and to meet and often address the various bodies interested in the United Nations, to endeavour to expedite the course of the Assembly's business so that it may wind up on the appointed closing date: all these are important and exacting functions.

As President I became acquainted with every relevant document. Of course I listened carefully to each speech in each Assembly debate. Some of them were long and properly so. The President cannot afford to nod. Naturally I knew the characteristics of each speaker and the approach he was likely to adopt. At the right moment, not easy to decide, I could suggest night meetings. An Assembly responds to strong leadership in debate. If I ruled somebody out of order, I had to be sure of my grounds. Presidents are rarely reversed on a point of order. It was my good fortune (my colleagues were always generous) never to be reversed.

But these tasks, although most important, are rather the

mechanics of the Presidency. What of the political responsibilities, of opportunities to reduce animosities, to pave the way toward settlements and to take part in them? I suppose every President commences his term of office with hopes of achieving some political results. How far he succeeds depends on himself, his aims, his experience, his courage, his standing before the Assembly, particularly his impartiality, and above all, his relations with the Secretary-General.

A President, however able and persuasive, cannot settle a problem where, for example, the West and the Communist bloc are poles apart; neither can the Secretary-General. The President may promote discussions but if, for example, on disarmament, the democracies and the Communists are profoundly divided, he will have to leave the removal of differences to the teeth of time and to the compelling urgencies of the nuclear world.

In disarmament I certainly tried, as I believe most of my predecessors did. I asked Vassili Kuznetsov, the Deputy Foreign Minister of the Soviet, to call on me. Nobody declines the President's call. Mr. Kuznetsov always treated me with complete courtesy and was the essence of punctuality. We saw each other alone. It would not be any breech of confidence on my part, since this was his public stand, to say that Mr. Kuznetsov considered that above all it was necessary, and that unconditionally, to cease nuclear testing. Everything was to flow from this. On the need for any conditions I found it impossible to persuade him. But I made the effort, not as the representative of a state but as the impartial President of the whole Assembly.

When I became President I ceased to take part in the deliberations of the New Zealand delegation or to attend any meetings of Commonwealth or other delegates. Although entitled to vote in the General Committee, I never exercised this prerogative. I did not enter the Delegates' Lounge. Of course I presided over weekly luncheons of committee chairmen, and I was always ready and anxious to see delegates who wished to discuss the Assembly's business. I would not see those who did not represent governments. Neither a President nor a Secretary-General will see the leader of a revolutionary movement.

One of my chief political occasions arose when the Syrian Foreign Minister, on October 15, 1957, complained in a letter to the Secretary-General that the movements of Turkish troops constituted "an actual military threat to Syria." On the following day Mr. Gromyko addressed to me a letter in which he set forth in detail his allegations of the nature and the extent of the Turkish forces near the Syrian frontier. He affirmed his government's belief "that the unleashing of the armed conflict that is being planned in that area by the ruling circles of Turkey and the United States is fraught with grave danger to the maintenance of general peace." Mr. Gromyko averred that the General Assembly without delay should consider the Syrian complaint.

These grave allegations were a threat to peace, and I felt that they should have gone to the Security Council first. However, I was asked to bring the matter before the Assembly. That could be done only through the General Committee which would or would not recommend to the Assembly that the Syrian complaint be inscribed on the Assembly's agenda. It was my function to decide when the General Committee, over which I presided, would meet.

On October 16, 1957, at about noon Salan Bitar, the Syrian

Minister of Foreign Affairs, called on me. He had first seen the Secretary-General. Mr. Bitar, who spoke in French, desired an immediate meeting of the General Committee. I pointed out that the Turkish government was entitled to consider the Syrian complaint and that a delay until October 17 was essential. Mr. Bitar readily agreed.

This was the very week of the visit of Queen Elizabeth II to Washington. As well as being President of the Assembly, I was Her Majesty's New Zealand Ambassador to the United States, and it was my honour and duty to meet the Queen when she arrived, with her husband the Duke of Edinburgh, in Washington on the morning of October 17. I duly did so and immediately flew back to New York, arriving before lunch. This meant that on the afternoon of October 17 I was unable to attend the Garden Party for the Queen in Washington where I was one of the hosts. With her invariable courtesy Her Majesty excused me. I felt it essential to be at the United Nations if there was to be a meeting of the General Committee in the afternoon. Also, I felt it was important that I should be seen in the United Nations buildings. I was unable to arrange a meeting of the General Committee until the afternoon of October 18. At the meeting Mr. Gromyko accused me of delaying the proceedings because I had been away in Washington, an allegation I, of course, immediately contradicted.

The General Committee decided to recommend the inscription of the Syrian item, and on the same afternoon the General Assembly adopted the recommendation. The Netherlands delegate made his point that the Security Council was the proper body to consider such a complaint in the first instance. Of course this was true. But as the days went by, it became clear that the Syrian item was a Soviet excursion into the cold war, in spite of the thunderous denunciations of Mr. Gromyko. He claimed that his government was in possession of Turkish invasion plans of Syria, but he never produced them. Many thought that the Russians were becoming more enthusiastic about the item, while the Syrians tended to cool off. I did not hesitate to tell the Syrian Foreign Minister that in my opinion his country had nothing to fear from the Turks and that the best way to reduce tension was not to put any resolution to vote. It seemed clear that neither of the resolutions before the Assembly would win the necessary two-thirds' majority.

The debate in the Assembly showed signs of petering out. The Arabs themselves seemed to feel that the Syrians were being used by the Soviet in the cold war. Finally one morning I was confronted with a meeting of the Assembly which it was hoped would end peacefully with no resolution being put to vote. It was essential to keep debate to a minimum. I had the good fortune to persuade one important delegate to refrain from speaking in spite of his government's instructions to the contrary. I was a relieved President when in an atmosphere of relaxation I could proceed to the next problem.

The Syrian item is an excellent example of the difficulties confronting a President and of the challenge to his capacity for handling men and controversies. I have heard it said on eminent authority that a diplomat who becomes President is "sterilised" during his term of office. This is far from true. He must intervene from time to time to exercise political functions although of course always with impartiality. He is not so active in this respect as the Secretary-General who, while he yields precedence to the President during the course of a session, has the advantage of continuous authority and in recent years of numerous functions delegated to him by the Assembly. My relations with the Secretary-General have always been excellent; during my Presidency we never encroached on each other's domain. Nevertheless, I could have wished for more information at certain stages of a controversy.

From time to time a President is asked to mediate. In a dispute affecting Abyssinia during my term of office it would have been normal to have asked either the President or the Secretary-General to be the arbitrator. But the Emperor of Abyssinia, belonging as he does to the family of monarchs, would have none of this. Accordingly, the King of Norway was chosen.

The President will always be an important official: as the titular head of the Assembly, its Chairman with far-reaching procedural responsibilities, and a composer of controversies. Like the Secretary-General, he has a lonely eminence and must work hard behind the scenes. I found my task a rewarding responsibility.

CHAPTER X

The Lonely Road of a Secretary-General

HISTORY IS FULL OF THE RECORDS OF POPES, EMPERORS, KINGS, presidents, prime ministers, generals, and despots. There have been only two Secretaries-General of the United Nations. Each has been able. It is no reflection on the great abilities of Trygve Lie to say that Dag Hammarskjold has attained a status which makes him like the greatest of the temporal popes, albeit without life tenure or a college of cardinals. But then many of the popes have ignored the consistory. The Secretary-General, although he must keep an anxious eye on the Great Powers, acts on his own responsibility within the Secretariat, which he dominates but which is in its own right one of the principal organs of the United Nations.

The physical area over which Dag Hammarskjold has jurisdiction in New York City is even smaller than that of Vatican City. But both Pope and Secretary-General exercise an influence far beyond their nominal powers. The Secretary-General holds office for a fixed term of five years, although in Mr. Hammarskjold's case it has been renewed. It is conceivable that in December, 1962, it again will be renewed. The field for the selection of Secretaries-General is small.

For some centuries it has been the custom for the Pope to be an Italian. Trygve Lie and Dag Hammarskjold are Scandinavians. For the foreseeable future it is safe to say that the Soviet will consent to the election of a Secretary-General only if he is a citizen of a country which is not a member of any of the Western defensive alliances. This would eliminate a Norwegian, a Dane, or an Icelander, but not a Swede. In fact, the Soviet Union never recognised the Assembly's one-year extension of Mr. Lie's original term. In Russian eyes he was guilty of two unpardonable sins: he was a citizen of Norway which became a member of NATO; in the Security Council he took an initiative against a Communist regime in 1950, when the forces of Northern Korea crossed the 38th parallel to invade Southern Korea.

Mr. Hammarskjold is a Swede of ancient lineage. Sweden is not a member of NATO or of any other Western defensive alliance. When the Security Council met in December, 1952, to recommend to the Assembly a successor to Mr. Lie, the first choice of the majority was Lester Pearson, the Canadian Minister of External Affairs. Although the Security Council proceeded by secret ballot, it is well known that the only, but decisive, vote against him was by the Soviet Union, which rejected Mr. Pearson because his country was a member of NATO.

While I deplored this, I recognised the validity of the principle that a Secretary-General must enjoy the confidence of all the Great Powers. This is indeed inherent in the terms of the Charter which provides that the Secretary-General shall be appointed by the Assembly on the recommendation of the Security Council. This provision confers the power of veto on any one of the permanent members of the Security

Council. The Russians used the veto against Mr. Pearson, although no one knew up to the last moment whether they would. This is their usual cat-and-mouse procedure.

During the drafting of the Charter, the conception of the mode of election of the Secretary-General had some transitions. At San Francisco the Soviet Union urged that he should be elected for a two-year term without the right to succeed himself, that these provisions should apply to his four deputies, and that he and his deputies all should be citizens of one or other of the Great Powers. This was consistent with the attitude of Stalin that the Great Powers by acting in unity would dominate the United Nations.

There was much debate over all these proposals. Some of the smaller powers favoured freer selection by the Assembly; the Soviet stood firm on the Yalta formula that conferred a veto to the Great Powers. Eventually the Soviet won, with the qualification that the Secretary-General be left to choose his chief aides. However, in practice he adheres to the principle of geographical distribution, and of his chief aides always one is an American and one a Russian.

When the Soviet rejected Lester Pearson, the situation became confused. The small powers had scant knowledge whom the permanent members of the Security Council proposed to nominate. Few delegates outside those from Europe knew Mr. Hammarskjold well. He was a delegate for his country in 1952, but in that position he conducted himself with customary reserve. I can still see him in the First Committee: cool, relaxed, reticent. Few, if any, saw Mr. Hammarskjold as the man who four years hence would speak in terms of authority to Britain and France.

I was informed of the proposal to elect him when the nomination was almost a *fait accompli*. There was need for speed and I have no particular quarrel with the method of selection save that I think there should have been more consultation. Even to Mr. Hammarskjold the election came as a complete surprise.

As soon as his qualifications were made known, there could be no doubt that he was a wise choice. He is a distinguished scholar and linguist, an economist well versed in the affairs of his country's Treasury and in European finances. He has been Under-Secretary of State to Sweden's Minister of Finance, Chairman for seven years of the Sveriges Riksbank, for three years Under-Secretary of State in the Swedish Ministry of Foreign Affairs. While not holding an elective office, he was a Swedish Minister of State from 1951 to 1953. By any count this is a most distinguished record.

He is a bachelor. I would not liken him to the most ascetic of the Popes but he is slender and elegant with a certain Renaissance subtlety not inconsistent with the priestly caste. There is no evidence that he likes the innumerable cocktail parties which afflict many delegates to the United Nations, and he is most discriminating in his attendance. He is a mountaineer and an apostle of modern art. He is a philosopher, a profound student of history and religion. He shuns publicity and is uncommunicative with the Press. In fact he prides himself on his skill and reticence before the fourth estate. He is a profound believer in quiet diplomacy. Indefatigable, in emergencies he proceeds for some days without sleep, as during the Suez crisis. He loves his position and is well aware of those, great and small, who seek to make use of him. He does not believe that the President of the Assembly has any power that competes with his own.

Once he had assumed office, Mr. Hammarskjold conducted himself, as always, with great circumspection. He had problems of personnel to deal with, because following his election the tentacles of McCarthyism reached into the Secretariat. He proved himself a strict upholder of the provision of the Charter whereby "each member of the United Nations undertakes to respect the exclusively international character of the responsibilities of the Secretary-General and his staff and not to seek to influence them in the discharge of their responsibilities." Today it seems a far cry from the time when there was a heresy hunt in the United States against some members of the Secretariat. Their impartiality is generally recognised.

I have dealt with the members of the Secretariat for over seven years. They come from all over the world, from civil services of differing standards and rules, some from undeveloped countries, some, of course, from the Communist states, as is inevitable, because the Charter provides that "due regard shall be paid to the importance of recruiting the staff on as wide a geographical basis as possible."

I have been impressed by the efficiency and the devotion to duty characteristic of members of the Secretariat. It is inevitable that there are varying standards, but I have no complaints concerning those who have served me. Indeed, I have nothing but gratitude toward them. The American, the Englishman, the Frenchman, the Indian, the South African, the Yugoslav, the Mexican, and the Canadian—and whoever else he may be—each as a detached and expert international civil servant has always informed and advised me.

Of course I shall be asked: what of the Russians in the Secretariat? The answer is that I have dealt with them only formally, and in the Security Council while I was President only on matters so simple as the settling of the list of speakers. It is the Secretary-General himself who deals with the Russians on matters of substance. That he should hear them obviously is his duty; that he should make his own decision after listening to advice from all quarters is his right.

If the Secretary-General has been chosen wisely, he can be trusted to keep a secret. This I believe to be altogether true of Mr. Hammarskjold as it was of Mr. Lie. On no other basis can the Secretary-General perform his office. There are Russians in the Secretariat and they have their right to certain appointments. They can approach and advise the Secretary-General. What he decides and what he chooses to communicate to others are his responsibility. For it must be remembered that above all the Secretary-General works alone. He has no equal in the Secretariat. He is perhaps the loneliest man in the world. He is the repository of many secrets. Mr. Hammarskjold can be trusted not to divulge such knowledge save to those entitled to receive it.

Article 99 of the Charter gives the Secretary-General a very significant power: he may bring to the attention of the Security Council any matter which, in his opinion, may threaten the maintenance of international peace and security. Under the League only a member state enjoyed this right. Under the Charter of the United Nations a single individual, the chosen of all the member states, may act if governments themselves are unwilling to do so. The United States delegation at San Francisco proposed that the Secretary-General could take a similar initiative before the Assembly. The proposal was not adopted. Nevertheless, when he believes peace to be threatened, the Secretary-General is ready to take the initiative in the Assembly as well as in the Security Council.

Mr. Lie used his initiative with some difficulty. In 1946, following the Russian withdrawal from the Iranian province of Azerbaijan, he intervened in the Security Council and asked that the matter be considered as concluded. Mr. Lie's intervention suited the Soviet, for its aim was to take the item off the agenda. In 1950, he acted immediately after the Northern Korean invasion of Southern Korea, thereby incurring the enmity of the Soviet. At the request of the United States representative, Mr. Lie convened the Security Council and when the meeting opened made the first statement, which he concluded by saying that it was the clear duty of the Security Council to take steps to re-establish peace in Korea. The indignation of the Soviet was not diminished by their mistake in absenting themselves from the Council meeting in which Mr. Lie had taken this bold initiative.

Mr. Hammarskjold, when he assumed office, thus had authority and precedent for taking initiative. But he was cautious. Even when he was thus disposed, I observed during New Zealand's tenure of office in the Security Council in 1954 and 1955 that neither Great Britain nor the United States seemed anxious to encourage him to act on his own accord. The Great Powers, virtually until the Suez crisis, regarded the great fields of diplomacy reserved for states and their representatives, not for an international official however eminent and whatever the terms of his mandate. The first breach in this attitude occurred in 1955 when the Assembly, on the initiative of the United States, requested Mr. Hammarskjold to go to Peking to secure the release of American prisoners of war then in Chinese hands.

This was a great task to entrust to a single individual, even though he had the prestige and the authority of the United Nations behind him. After all, Communist China was not in the world organization. There was an armistice in Korea. Unwilling to risk another conflict, the United States was ready to use the services of the world's chief civil servant. From the time he set forth on his mission to Peking and particularly later, after certain prisoners were released, Mr. Hammarskjold began to attain a stature and influence which have grown steadily, but never so rapidly as during and after the Suez crisis.

The task of clearing the canal was entrusted to him and the experts whom he chose to select. He had the major responsibility for creating the United Nations Emergency Force, although he had the benefit of an Advisory Committee established by the Assembly. The Force is subject to his control, although in this respect he remains the servant of the Assembly. These developments involved great powers and responsibilities, and they have encouraged Mr. Hammarskjold to act or refrain from acting.

It is interesting to study his own language when acting during a particular situation and more so because his words are far from easy to follow and illustrate his turn of mind:

> Without discussing the decisive importance of the national policy of member states for the solution of, let us say, the Suez crisis, I should like to recall that the success of the policy followed was predicated on the specific possibilities of shaping an organized cooperation within the universal UN framework. Furthermore, only through this organization was it possible to create the police force—the UNEF—without which things would have developed quite differently, and probably catastrophically.

This is the Secretary-General's rather obscure way of saying that working in close co-operation with his Advisory Committee and with the Foreign Minister of Egypt he succeeded in creating the Emergency Force. Here he revealed his capacities for continuous hard work, adaptability, patience, and courage. For in many cases the resolutions of the Assembly giving him authority were vague and incomplete, the Great Powers were unable or unwilling to give more precise authority, and the Secretary-General filled a vacuum by acting, occasionally making a statement of policy, which nobody questioned, from his seat beside the President.

During the Lebanese and Jordan crises of 1958 he took initiatives both in the Security Council and in the Assembly. He announced to the Council that he would increase the number of observers in Lebanon, and no member objected. Probably most members were aware that he intended to do this, but the step was the move of the Secretary-General.

Then came the Emergency Session of the Assembly which met in August, 1958, over which I presided. At the opening of that Assembly Mr. Hammarskjold read a statement outlining his policy and views on the Middle East. He had not done this without consultation in important quarters. Even allowing for these preliminary soundings, it was a bold thing to do and amounted to the Secretary-General taking initiative before the Assembly, something which the Charter does not specifically give him. When proposed at San Francisco, it was thought to involve a substantial change in the Secretary-General's functions.

Shortly after the Secretary-General's opening statement to the Emergency Session, the President of the United States addressed the Assembly. Among other points Mr. Eisenhower proposed the creation of a permanent peace force. The proposal fell on stony ground and there is considerable evidence that it "was quietly side-stepped at the instigation of the Secretary-General." Certainly no more was heard of it at the Assembly which followed swiftly on the heels of the Emergency Session. The Secretary-General is now powerful enough to bury a proposal, although first he must be sure of considerable support.

The increase in his powers derives from Suez mainly because the Great Powers either have been unable to agree among themselves or have been unwilling to discharge certain responsibilities in the Middle East. Under these circumstances they ask the Secretary-General to explore the possibilities of action and to report to the Assembly or to take steps.

This is an entirely novel state of affairs. It is impossible to imagine the Great Powers after 1815 or indeed after 1918 devolving major political responsibilities upon a single international civil servant. Is this a good thing? Given the circumstances, I think so. There seems to be no likelihood of the United States and Great Britain on the one side and the Soviet on the other reaching a common policy on the Middle East. Nor do the United States and Great Britain appear ready, if that even were wise, to adopt any policy of pressure in the area to produce a settlement of the Arab-Israeli problem. It seems inevitable, therefore, that with a Secretary-General able and willing to exercise his influence and to use his right of initiative, the Assembly, inspired by the Great Powers, will ask him to discharge important tasks, both in the Middle East and elsewhere.

Mr. Hammarskjold does such work with great wisdom, patience, and skill. He is an apostle of gradualness and is content if he succeeds step by step. He has acquired an immense and unique knowledge and influence in the service of the United Nations. The problem is whether a successor could be found with like attainments and experience, given the fact that the Russians will not accept a Secretary-General save from a noncommitteed country. In practice this means that Mr. Hammarskjold's successor must be chosen from Sweden, Finland, Switzerland, or India. This is a far from satisfactory position. Granted that the Secretary-General should have the confidence of all the Great Powers, it is a matter for concern that one of them should exercise a veto for the purpose of ensuring that the chief servant of the United Nations be selected solely from a country detached from the democracies' defensive alliances.

CHAPTER XI

Our Window on the Russian Mind

. . . Lenin proved only a partially successful inno-
vator. He had to conform to the permanent and
indestructible forces in Russia. He illustrated the
maxim that it is the differences and not the resem-
blances between Russia and the West, which are
really important in Russian history . . . the vigour
of the Russian Revolution and its increasing power
depend neither on personality nor on machinery as
such. They depend on the character of the Russian
masses, which is moved and propelled by ideas and
influences alien to the West. . . . Russia has, in fact,
never resembled the West, though at times she has
taken lessons from it.

—*Europe in the Nineteenth and Twentieth Centuries*
by Grant and Temperley

When the animals met to discuss disarmament, the
Lion looked the Eagle in the eye and said, "We must
abolish talons!" The Eagle looked squarely into the
Lion's eye and said, "We must abolish claws." Then
the Bear said, "Let's abolish everything except universal embraces."

—Salvador de Madariaga (1932)

IT IS THE CONSTANT FEAR OF "UNIVERSAL EMBRACES" FROM THE
bear which oppresses the Western world today and afflicts

113

the United Nations. The world organization *is* plagued by the division of the world between the Communist states and the democracies. The hard reality, which we would obscure at our peril, is that the United Nations must do its work in a divided world, a world in which mankind for too long has been without dependable safeguards against the catastrophe of total war.

As I see it, and my tenure of office as President of the Twelfth Assembly has confirmed my belief, this division of the world and the ideological struggle from which it grows remain the central issue, overshadowing all others. This division, with its complex of action and reaction, its combination of pressure and resistance, of threat and counterthreat, has, since 1946, reduced the effectiveness of the United Nations, particularly through the veto of the Security Council, and restricted the capacity of the organization to realise its Charter potentialities. It has jeopardised the security of the uncommitted no less than the contestants and made them all its victims. It has given local and regional disputes a universal significance, perpetuating old antagonisms, creating new ones, complicating the solutions. Its consequences are not circumscribed; they range beyond the domain of politics, multiplying controversy even at the limits of intergovernmental contact.

But its corrosive effects are felt most directly in the political arena, and therefore in all the organs of the United Nations. This has been so at all sessions of the Assembly and as President of the Twelfth I did not escape its consequences. Nothing gave me a greater feeling of frustration than my failure to break through Russian intransigence on the question of disarmament. In the previous five years in my various capacities as President of the Trusteeship Council, of the Security Council, and as Chairman of the First Committee, I had ample experience with the undeviating line taken by the Russians on various problems. But as President of the Assembly, when the issues posed by disarmament in the nuclear age cried for an urgent solution, I had hoped than an appeal to the Russians for a compromise would have some effect. I had no success.

What then is the nature of the Russians? Few people, whether admirers or detractors, understand the Russians, their motives and characteristics. The proportion of people in any country who have travelled in Russia is very small. Those outside the Communist world who can speak Russian are few, although fortunately their number is increasing. In Britain and the United States there is probably a far greater knowledge of the history of France than of Russia, although Russia, as the leader of the Communist world, is a mighty expanding force, which only the United States can surpass—some might say equal.

Few appreciate the impact of climate, geography, and history upon the Russian. It is important to remember the long and harsh winter, the illimitable steppes, and the isolation from outside contacts forced upon him by the Tsars, only recently modified by his Communist rulers. Consider the influence of the Tatars on customs and race, the complete absence of democracy both under Tsars and Communists, a Byzantine regime based upon centuries of serfdom with the peasant still dragooned into collective farms, the close identity of state and an acquiescent church under the Tsars, and Communist contempt for religion. Then came the fearful ordeal of the German invasion with an appalling Russian loss of 16,000,000 people. These are some of the factors producing a nation almost as much Asian as European, accustomed to suffering and autocracy, patriotic, brave, long-suffering, patient, suspicious, ignorant of the outside world. Although in the grasp of the Communist machine, it is conscious and proud of making immense strides in science and engineering.

From my dealings with the Russians in the United Nations I have always thought that our greatest danger in the West lay in underestimating them. I shall never forget the astonishment of many delegations, shared by numerous newspapers in the United States, when the Russians first sent a Sputnik into outer space. Too many in the West had believed for too long that Communist rule was fatal to great scientific attainments. It was a rude but salutary shock, having an element of comfort. The immense material progress of the Soviet Union since the Revolution stems from a growing class of managers and technicians who must desire security for themselves and their families. Indispensable to the Soviet regime, they have special privileges. If they are to serve their country, they must be free from the anxiety of recurring purges. We have some justification for hoping that this expert class will set a brake on the ambitions of the Communist bosses.

The chief opportunity for the average diplomat to get some direct knowledge of the Russians is by a tour of duty at the United Nations. I except those, of course, who are appointed to Moscow, but they are comparatively few; many governments have no diplomatic representation in Russia. Many Americans have expressed their disapproval of Russian membership in the United Nations, particularly because of the opportunity given for constant Communist propaganda. I believe this disapproval to be quite mistaken.

The United Nations provides an indispensable window into the Russian mind. More people in the Western world than some of us realise have understood little of the meaning of communism, its aims and methods. The television of UN proceedings and the Press have given them some idea of the obstinacy of the Communist diplomat, of his constant assertion of Russian virtue in every controversy and of the wickedness of Wall Street and its "warmongers," of the incredible mendacity which, day in, day out, accused the Americans of germ warfare in Northern Korea, of the ceaseless denunciation of colonialism, while Eastern Europe is in the iron grip of the Russian Army. The intelligent observer of television has the opportunity to realise the great ability of many Russian diplomats and their tireless devotion to the cause of imperialistic communism.

Those who watch the debates of the United Nations should remember that the Soviet diplomats are a very specialised class of the Russian people. True, for the most part they come from ordinary ranks and in some cases from the poorest. But they all appear to be dedicated and trained Communists, carefully selected, carefully watched. Some have avowed their gratitude to the Party which has raised them from obscurity to eminence. They are genial when the word from Moscow is for geniality, dour when the instruction to diplomats is for dourness. I shall never forget the change following the death of Stalin.

We learned of his demise one morning in the First Committee. Vishinsky was greatly affected and I think genuinely, because as a Menshevik his tenure of office was said to be based on Stalin's goodwill. But there was Vishinsky in tears. From that day onward, with the rise of Nikita Khrushchev, who knows how to smile, the Soviet diplomats at the United Nations unbent.

But whether genial or dour, the Soviet diplomats are members of the Communist Party, which is only a very small proportion of the Russian people. The Communist Party has, of course, to a degree indoctrinated the nation; in particular under Lenin and Stalin it has erected such a barrier between Russia and the West that most Russians, however inquiring their minds, have little knowledge of and often prejudices against the United States. We would be wrong, however, to forget that not even the Communist Party can destroy the great qualities of the Russian people, qualities which make their country one of the strongest in the modern world.

On the conclusion of hostilities a Russian general remarked to an American colleague that demobilization was a headache to the Soviet: it gave the man in the ranks knowledge of the amenities of the West.

Until I came to the United Nations in February, 1952, my knowledge of the Russians was derived from histories of the Tsars and of the Revolution. I had received a deep impression from the sombre words of Winston Churchill depicting the crumbling of the Eastern front in the First World War, the massacre of the Imperial family, and the sinister struggle for power between Stalin and Trotsky.

It was therefore in no mood of optimism that I met the Russian delegation to the Trusteeship Council, headed by Arkady A. Soldatov, an experienced historian and philologist and today head of the American department of the Soviet Foreign Ministry. Incidentally, he is an important

and pleasant person. Subsequently I was to deal with Andrei
Vishinsky, Vyacheslav Molotov, Andrei A. Gromyko, Ar-
kady A. Sobolev, Vassili Kuznetsov, Georgi N. Zarubin, and
Mikhail Menshikov. Of them, only Molotov was ever in the
very front seat of power in Moscow, but they all implemented
Russian foreign policy.

All conform to a pattern, and it is proper to say that I never
got close to any Russian diplomat. I do not know any Western
diplomat who has. In the first place, they are all hard-work-
ing. In fact, their industry is depressing. Most of them show
considerable versatility. Many have been in other walks of
life, particularly in science and engineering, before entering
the field of diplomacy.

Vishinsky had been a professor of criminal law at the University of Moscow and was a foremost authority on the theory
and practice of the Soviet legal system. Those who crossed
swords with him without knowing their facts suffered. He
was a remorseless and unscrupulous debater. Yet with all
this and with the full knowledge of his part in the celebrated
treason trials of 1936–1938, I found it impossible not to pay
tribute to his great ability and personality. He was one of
the "characters" of the United Nations.

Molotov was the most forbidding of them. To paraphrase
Sir Harold Nicolson, looking into Molotov's eyes was like
looking into a refrigerator which had all its lights extin-
guished.

Gromyko came from a scientific background and at one
time had been a senior scientific worker in the Economic In-
stitute. An eminent American statesman has described Gromyko as the ablest technician in diplomacy he knew. He is
dour and uncompromising; I have never detected in Gromyko

any goodwill toward the West or any disposition to believe in the goodwill of a United States administration. During my Presidency of the Twelfth Assembly, I had the temerity to interrupt him when I thought he was straying from the point. He turned on me with a ferocity which would have alarmed me had I been in his power. This is perhaps not altogether surprising, given the Soviet approach toward power. I come from a country with a population of two and a quarter million people. Mr. Gromyko represented a mighty state with a population of two hundred million. Did not Mr. Stalin at Teheran ask how many divisions were at the disposition of the Pope? Moreover, many Russians do not understand the constitutional position of the independent states of the members of the Commonwealth and are apt to attribute the same degree of independence to New Zealand as they would accord, shall we say, to Roumania vis-à-vis themselves. Formerly, when the New Zealand representative expressed himself on certain problems, the privilege of replying to him was accorded to the representative of Byelorussia. I always regarded it as a sign of my increasing importance when the Soviet representative himself referred on occasion to my views, not by any means by way of approbation. However distasteful his manner, Gromyko has a competency and a reserve which are impressive. I believe that although he is Foreign Minister, he is not in the supreme councils of Soviet power and that he may not be so influential as Kuznetsov, who is one of his deputies. In the Soviet system a deputy may have more power than his nominal chief; a counsellor or first secretary in a Soviet Embassy may have more influence with Moscow than the Ambassador, especially if the counsellor or secretary is a member of the Secret Police.

Kuznetsov, seemingly the most sincere of all the Russian diplomats whom I know, was at one time an exchange student in the United States and worked in the Ford River Rouge plant. For eight years he was Chairman of the Soviet All Union Central Committee of Trade Unions. Then he entered the Foreign Office, was Ambassador in Peking, and is now a Deputy Foreign Minister. As unyielding as his colleagues, he rather alleviates this by his earnestness. Like most Russian diplomats, he has an abiding fear of a resurgent Germany, born of a vivid recollection of Russian sufferings in the Second World War. If any Russian should be aware of the nonaggressive character of the American people it should be Kuznetsov. I have taken him to the window of my suite, pointed to Long Island, and said "Do you really believe, Mr. Kuznetsov, these people want war?" He agreed that they did not, but then harked back to the warmongers in other quarters.

Like Kuznetsov, the late Zarubin had been an engineer. A favorite gambit with Zarubin, who died in December, 1958, was that he would have much preferred to remain an engineer. It is generally believed that he had been a member of the Soviet Secret Police. Some found him dour and forbidding, but that was not my experience. During my dealings with him in New York and Washington I found him tough, but when as Chairman of a committee I made rulings, he never showed any ill will after he had tried unsuccessfully to secure a vote reversing me. I can best illustrate this aspect of his character by describing my experience as Chairman of the Credentials Committee, which has the duty of recommending to the Assembly the approval or otherwise of the various delegates' letters of appointment. As a rule this is a formal procedure, but in the case of China it has involved a yearly controversy as to who is entitled to represent China in the United Nations, with the United States the successful protagonist of the view that the legitimate government of China is that headed by Generalissimo Chiang Kai-shek whose capital is in Formosa.

In the opening days of the session of the Assembly, the United States invariably introduces the so-called "moratorium" resolution whereby the Assembly decides not to consider at its regular session any proposal to exclude the representatives of the government of the Republic of China or to seat representatives of the Central People's government of the People's Republic of China. After an acrimonious debate in the General Committee and the Assembly, in which the leading protagonists for some years have been Henry Cabot Lodge and a Soviet Foreign Minister, the American proposal is put to the vote and carried by a majority of about twenty. Those who vote against the proposal are the nine members of the Communist bloc, the five members of the Scandinavian bloc (Norway, Sweden, Finland, Denmark, and Iceland) and a majority of those in the Afro-Asian bloc, led on this subject by India.

At some stage in the Session, usually late, the Credentials Committee meets and the Soviet delegate invariably claims that the only true representative of China is the People's government of China. As the matter has been dealt with by the moratorium procedure, the Chairman invariably rules the Soviet proposal out of order and invariably he is upheld. I was Chairman of this Committee on two occasions when Mr. Zarubin represented the Soviet Union. He never bore me any ill will because of my ruling, resolutely and decisively as I made it. After the first of the Credentials Committee meetings he always cheerfully greeted me in the corridors with the title "Boss."

Like all other delegates, the Soviet representatives are voting on instructions. They are tough fighters, but they are entitled to be. Frequently I have dealt with them on points of procedure; when they have given me their word, they have adhered to it as I have to mine. Of course we have been miles apart on points of substance resulting from the division between the democracies and the Communists. I can never make up my mind whether the Communist representatives really believe in the patent absurdities which they utter so blatantly. They speak of their solicitude for the rights of small nations, while the record shows the fate of the Baltic States. They denounce what they call Anglo-French aggression against Egypt, blandly ignoring their own invasion of Hungary. Like Goebbels, they probably believe that by constant reiteration of a lie many people may come to believe it. And certainly among Asians—not by any means all—there was much greater indignation over Suez than over Hungary.

The methods of the autocracy of Khrushchev are not different in principle from those of the Tsars. As a Russian prince observed to the Frenchman, the Marquis de Custine in 1839, "Russian despotism not only counts ideas and sentiments for nothing but remakes facts; it wages war on evidence and triumphs in the battle. . . . For evidence has no defender in Russia, no more than justice when they embarrass the power."

The Party line is, of course, rigidly followed by all the representatives of the satellites, with the Poles alone, frequently with great courage, speaking on occasion in rather muted tones. On some subjects, indeed, the Bulgarian may speak at greater length and with more wearisome repetition than even the Soviet. But he is apt to address a very thin audience.

How then are we to deal with the Russians in the United Nations? We must persist, both inside and outside the United Nations, in presenting the Western case and in attempting to settle the many problems which produce such a state of tension today and which, unresolved, could lead to war. Persistence on our side has led to results after disheartening delays, as shown by the conclusion of an armistice in Korea and the Austrian peace treaty.

Moreover, it sometimes happens that after the Russians most strongly denounce a proposal, they suddenly adopt it and claim it as their own. I do not consider that they are anxious for a general war, which, whether they won or lost, would certainly wreck their country and the system which they have so laboriously constructed since the Revolution.

We must ceaselessly strive for the spread of cultural contacts between Russia and the West and for visits of the ordinary folk of Russia to the West. For we must never forget, as de Custine pointed out over a century ago that "Russia alone, belatedly civilised, has been deprived of a profound fermentation and of the benefit of a slow and natural cultural development, because of the impatience of her leaders."

Our chief anxiety must be over Soviet attempts to divide the West, particularly the United States, the United Kingdom, France, and Western Germany. This is no doubt what they are attempting to achieve by their proposals for the establishment of a "free" Berlin. Another anxiety for the West must be Communist probings at the periphery with the danger of limited wars spreading into a conflagration.

That the Communists will exploit our divisions and our weaknesses in the Middle and Far East is obvious.

These conclusions emphasise the importance of the United Nations and its various instruments, including, of course, the Secretary-General, as means for debate, negotiation, and pacification. The Foreign Minister of Ireland, Frank Aiken, had some very wise words to say in the Twelfth Assembly in the course of the disarmament debate:

> Where there is a vital conflict of interests, or mutual fear of deadly violence, between two sets of human beings, peace can only be maintained in one or two ways: by the acceptance of the rule of law or by the superior force of a third party. We are all now in the inescapable dilemma that we have no third party except the collective judgment of mankind represented in this Assembly: unless we now make rapid progress towards the rule of law, we may soon have drifted past the lost opportunity to prevent the use of ultimate weapons.

CHAPTER XII

The Perils of Middle East Conflict

OF ALL MY WORK IN THE UNITED NATIONS NONE HAS OCCUPIED my attention more than the Arab-Israeli problem. From 1952 to 1958 I have participated or presided in debates on it either in the Security Council or in the Assembly.

In November, 1947, the General Assembly made a decision which changed the face of the Middle East, a decision affecting not only the Middle East but the whole community of nations. Its consequences fashioned the destiny of millions who are likely to be a major concern to the world for years to come.

The Palestine problem was first brought to the Assembly in February, 1947. In November of that year, when the General Assembly adopted its resolution on Palestine, New Zealand was among the majority of countries which voted affirmatively. This resolution approved the plan to terminate the British mandate and to create a Jewish state and an Arab state to be federated economically, as well as to set up a special international regime—a *corpus separatum*—for the city of Jerusalem. This plan of partition with economic union was not arrived at lightly; nor was it endorsed capriciously by New Zealand or any other member of the Assembly, but only after the most searching scrutiny of all the alternatives.

I recall the comment the leader of the New Zealand delegation made to the 1947 Assembly:

> No one could, and no one did, doubt the moral and logical cogency of many of the arguments advanced by the representatives of the Arab states in opposition to partition. But the tangled conflict of admitted rights and wrongs of both sides had been most carefully and anxiously and honestly weighed. . . . The decision was considered to be that which was open to the least objection, which created less injustice than any other possible solution and offered the best prospects of a final settlement of a most intractable problem.

New Zealand therefore supported the principle of partition; but we entertained the most lively apprehensions over the failure of the Assembly to provide adequate means of endorsing partition. We believed that if the United Nations assumed the responsibility for the partition of Palestine, it simultaneously should assume the duty of protecting the population of Palestine against any resulting disturbance. We did not conceal our fear that the vacuum created by the withdrawal of the mandatory power would be filled by chaos and violence unless the United Nations took preventive action. All were aware of tension in the mandate and of Arab hostility to partition.

For this reason, New Zealand pressed strongly in the Assembly for an understanding that all members of the United Nations, especially the permanent members of the Security Council, would be ready, if the need arose, to implement the plan of partition by means of an international force to which all would contribute in proportion to their strength. The idea of an international force is not new.

Unhappily, this plea went unheeded. During the transitional period before the termination of the British mandate, guerilla war and anarchy reigned in Palestine. The Palestine Commission did not get from the Security Council the armed assistance it needed if partition was to be effected without widespread violence. The United Kingdom, the mandatory power was unwilling to take upon itself the onus of enforcing a plan which had not been found acceptable both to the Arab and the Jewish communities.

When the Assembly met in special session in April, 1948, it had before it a report of the Palestine Commission which conveyed the warning that "in the absence of forces adequate to restore and maintain order in Palestine following the termination of the Mandate, there will be administrative chaos, starvation, widespread strife, violence and bloodshed in Palestine."

The organization's response to this warning fell short of the necessities of the situation. In effect, the United Nations left the solution to the arbitrament of war, which was waged bitterly between the Arabs and the new state of Israel which had been officially proclaimed on May 14, 1948.

The war in Palestine meant the violent setting aside of the United Nations plan for two independent states, one Jewish and one Arab in the Holy Land, and for the internationalisation of Jerusalem. Israel emerged with a larger share of the former mandated territory than originally allocated to her. The rest of the area was occupied by the Arab countries. Jerusalem became partly Israeli, partly Jordanian.

The war had other effects. It brought not only destruction

and death but flight and evacuation. Perhaps the most tragic of all its consequences was the exodus of almost a million Palestinian Arabs to neighbouring Arab lands. The prolongation of the refugee issue had been, both in human and political terms, the most harassing aspect of the Palestine question.

The unsolved Palestine problem has been and is likely to remain of deep and recurring concern in the United Nations forum. In the Middle East it has deprived neighbours of the opportunity to co-operate in joint measures which the welfare of their area demands. Instead, both parties have journeyed far along the road of enmity and conflict. For years the situation has been one of armed vigilance, of open and covert violence, of blockade and boycott, raid and reprisal. In an area whose security is of far more than regional significance, the threat of war is constant. This has meant a disastrous competition in armaments and a diversion of resources desperately needed to combat poverty and disease. It has meant dislocation in commerce, communications, and economic development, and a heavy mutual loss of benefits from joint exploitation of natural wealth. It has encouraged political extremism and has multiplied opportunities for penetration by forces of international communism. And it has condemned over 900,000 Arab refugees to long years of misery.

How has the United Nations sought to promote a settlement? The organization has worked on the problem in three interrelated ways: its first concern has been with the maintenance of peace and compliance with the Armistice Agreements reached in 1949 between Israel and her immediate neighbours: Egypt, Syria, Lebanon, and Jordan. Since 1949 the Armistice regime, established through the United Nations, has been the constant preoccupation of the Security

Council and the Truce Supervision Organization operating in the area.

In spite of the painstaking work of the Truce Supervision Organization, up to 1956 the situation grew worse, with border raids and planned retaliation occurring on an increasingly ominous scale. None will forget the events of October and November, 1956. The Assembly's intervention led to the withdrawal of British, French, and Israeli forces from Egyptian territory and to the formation of the United Nations Emergency Force. But the cessation of hostilities was not accompanied by a solution to the problems of the Middle East. UNEF is no more than a restraint.

The urgent requirement is a transition from an uneasy truce to a permanent settlement. In this, which might be termed the second line of United Nations endeavour, the results have been meagre. The problems are admittedly of peculiar difficulty. But the last full-scale United Nations examination of the fundamental issues was as long ago as 1952, when the Assembly considered the work of the Palestine Conciliation Commission. The Commission was obliged to report that it had been unable to secure the two parties' full use of the mediatory facilities it had to offer them.

Many speakers in the debate noted that direct negotiations between the parties had been effective in the conclusion of the Armistice Agreement. It was therefore suggested that direct negotiations for a settlement of all outstanding differences should be begun. The Arab response, however, was that the Assembly should endorse, as a basis for negotiations, their interpretation of earlier Assembly resolutions. This would have committed Israel to accept the return of all Arab refugees to Israel and to withdraw to the boundaries established for it under the original partition plan. For its part, Israel reaffirmed its desire to enter into direct negotiations, but it put forward a peace proposal involving a considerable departure from previous Assembly resolutions. The Assembly failed to adopt any of the resolutions put before it, because none attracted the necessary two-thirds' majority.

I would like to emphasise a viewpoint I expressed in the 1952 debate and again in 1957, during the Eleventh Assembly. Clearly, the United Nations cannot be expected to play a decisive role in solving the Palestine problem: that role remains to be assumed by the two parties directly concerned. But it cannot, as a world peace organization, afford to divest itself of its responsibility to assist in the search for a settlement. It was with this in mind that I affirmed my government's hope that there would be no complacent assumption that Israel's withdrawal from Egyptian territory and the creation of more stable conditions along the frontier would mark the end of the Assembly's task. This is what I said:

> The Assembly cannot, admittedly, impose a permanent solution. Any settlement which is to last must be freely accepted by the parties; it would be a fatal mistake, however, to deduce from this that the United Nations is obliged to stand back and do nothing merely because an acceptable solution does not seem in sight. The dangers of a policy of drift have been amply demonstrated by the explosion of pent-up violence which occurred last October. Only a negotiated settlement will prevent a second tragedy.

I have always regretted that in 1956 no efforts were made to implement a draft resolution for the formulation of proposals for a lasting political settlement. When he spoke in the 1952 debate, Ambassador Eban of Israel observed that "peace with Israel is a debt which the Arab countries owe to history and the world." I must confess that I am led to wonder, when I study the record, whether this peace, which is so earnestly besought and so urgently needed, is not sometimes regarded as a peace whose terms admit of no compromise. I firmly believe that peace on mutually acceptable terms is a debt which both parties, both Israel and the Arab countries owe to each other, to history, and to the world.

I say this in full awareness of the Arab attitude toward Israel. I can understand why that attitude is held, but with the best will in the world I cannot regard it as conducive to a reconciliation on any realistic terms. Israel is an independent, sovereign state. It has been recognised as such by a large number of other sovereign governments. It is a member of the United Nations. Israel cannot be wished out of existence; nor can the Palestine of 1947 be restored by an act of will.

I speak with my Security Council experience in mind when I say there can be no room for a posture of offence, of bellicose vigilance, which anticipates trouble before it strikes and converts minor incidents into major crises. Policies of boycott and blockade are not compatible with peaceful economic intercourse. The spirit of the Armistice Agreement with Israel is violated and the freedom of international navigation is infringed if Israel's shipping is denied free and peaceful access to the Suez Canal. Finally, there can be no peace settlement if the Arab governments maintain their refusal to sit down and talk peace with Israel. The will to peace cannot be confined to one party. It must be accompanied by a readiness to compromise on the part both of Israel and of the Arabs.

Adjustments and concessions may be painful; but until the offer is made, we do not know whether it will be rejected. And unless it *is* made, in a demonstrable spirit of sincerity, it is hard to see how there can be any coming together.

I am well aware of the tendency on both sides to say: "If you are not with us, you must be against us." Advice need not always be bad to be resented. From the beginning, deep passions have been aroused; blood has been spilt; justified grievances have remained unredressed; and time has been no healer. But from the beginning, if I may venture the opinion, there have been serious shortcomings and serious omissions on *both* sides. There have, admittedly, been gradations of error and varying degrees of culpability. But one thing is clear: there will be no solution if each side continues to insist that all the blame must be borne by the other.

The conflict of policy on the two main issues can be stated briefly:

With regard to the *territorial* question, the Arab governments insist that the partition resolution should be implemented. This would require Israel to evacuate about 2,000 square miles (principally in the Negev) of what originally was intended to be Arab territory. Israel's position is that it is unreal to seek to revive the 1947 resolution which the Arab states opposed by force. Instead, she proposes a territorial settlement based on the existing Armistice lines, with frontier adjustments to be effected in mutually agreed particulars.

The second issue concerns the Arab refugees. In the absence of a permanent settlement, the care of refugees has fallen to the United Nations organization; and it is in discharging this humanitarian task that the United Nations has pursued its third line of endeavour in the Arab-Israeli dispute.

The refugee problem is the most complex and most distressing of all the issues which combine to divide Israel from her Arab neighbours. The Assembly has set up an Agency, known as UNRWA, which depends on voluntary contributions from governments. By far the largest contributor is the United States government, which has for a number of years provided 70 per cent of UNRWA's modest budget. Other substantial contributions have come from the United Kingdom, Canada, France, Australia, and New Zealand. Only a small proportion of members are contributors.

The Agency has suffered increasingly from a shortage of funds; and in spite of the magnificent and devoted work of its recent Director, Henry Labouisse, and his staff, it has been unable to do much more than keep the unfortunate refugees alive. Their physical and mental condition is pitiable. For them, the war of 1948 has brought only misery, deprivation, and degradation. There are now over 900,000 of them, in the Gaza Strip, Jordan, Lebanon, and Syria; and their numbers are constantly growing.

The member nations of the Assembly can, I believe, be under no illusion about the consequences of any failure on their part to give UNRWA the funds it needs to continue its humanitarian work. Let it be remembered that in 1960 UNRWA is to be terminated, although this seems unthinkable. At the Twelfth Assembly, Mr. Labouisse emphasised that the Agency could never be a substitute for political decisions and actions that ultimately must be taken by the governments concerned with the refugee problem. But he pointed out—and this is an important truth—that UNRWA is one of the prices, perhaps the cheapest, that the United Nations is paying for not being able to solve with equity the political problem of the Palestine refugees. UNRWA, he said, was helping, as was UNEF, to maintain an atmosphere of relative calm in which a solution could be sought. If the Assembly failed to provide the needed funds, it would be creating a situation which might lead not only to greater human suffering but also to renewed unrest in the whole area.

As President, I considered it my duty to lend unqualified support to UNRWA. As I told the Assembly, UNRWA's plight presented a serious challenge to the United Nations. I said then, and firmly believe now, that the United Nations cannot possibly allow the Agency's work to fail. There is too much at stake; and I am confident that member governments are fully aware of this.

Now what of the political problem and the attitudes of the parties directly concerned? The Arab countries have refused to contemplate any other course but the return of the refugees to their former homes. This, they say, is the unanimous wish of the refugees themselves, who maintain their collective claim that a grave injustice has been done. All the resolutions adopted by the Assembly on the subject of the refugees have affirmed the refugees' right to be repatriated or to be compensated for the property they left behind in Israel. The principle of repatriation must, in the Arab view, be accepted by Israel before there can be any talk of a peace settlement. Israel, moreover, in the Arab belief, is obliged, as a matter of law and justice, to pay the refugees for the lands and property that have been taken from them.

The Israeli proposals for a solution are based on a totally divergent point of view, which rejects the possibility of large-scale repatriation. Israel contends that the Arab states must be held responsible for creating the refugee problem, for perpetuating it, and for frustrating its solution. The root of the problem, as Israeli spokesmen have presented it, is Arab belligerency, obsessive Arab hatred of Israel, and the refusal of Arab leaders to adjust their policies to the needs of the refugees as human beings rather than to the needs of their vendetta against Israel. The only answer, according to Israel, is the integration and settlement of the refugees in Arab lands. But permanent resettlement, for which ample international aid was available, has been systematically blocked, according to Israel, by organized refugee intransigence and official Arab opposition. It is contended that if Israel, with its small territory and meagre resources, could absorb almost a million newcomers in nine years, the Arab countries, with their expanding economies, could easily find homes for a similar number in their own more spacious territories.

These are the attitudes providing the background to many bitter and fruitless debates in the United Nations. While the deadlock has continued, the refugees, the victims of a predicament not of their own making, are condemned to live, without dignity and hope, as the wards of the international community. No one who is familiar with this tragic issue of the Arab refugees would want to minimise its difficulties and complexities.

It is pointless to say that the problem would be solved if only one side or the other would take some uncomplicated step: we must all seek to avoid the temptation to prescribe facile remedies for this or the other vexed elements of the dispute. And it is in that respect that the positions adopted by the parties are open to the greatest criticism: they have the merit of simplicity; but they also have the fatal demerit of being completely irreconcilable. The answer is not to be found either in the total repudiation of the principle of repatriation or insistence of the mass re-absorption of the refugees into Israel.

I agree with the observation of the Saudi-Arabian representative at the Thirteenth Assembly that "the refugees are there, and the problem is there, no matter who is innocent and who is guilty." By the terms of a resolution of the Assembly the refugees are entitled to a choice—repatriation for those who seek to return in peace to their homes, compensation for those who decide to do otherwise. Notwithstanding difficulties of resettlement and problems of security, I believe that Israel would be wise to offer to take back a significant number of refugees.

I cannot believe that Arab and Israeli statesmanship will not be drawn to recognise that both parties must seek to come together on this as on their other problems. On the one hand there is a nation of a generous spirit, a people who have themselves had the harshest experience of persecution and blind fanaticism, who know themselves what it is to be a refugee. On the other hand is a proud and ancient race which stands in need of peace and the opportunity to free its people from poverty and want, which are the ancient enemies of mankind. In this area, as in the world at large, the peaceful challenges are enormous; it is tragic that fear and hostility should impair the joint capacity to face those challenges.

I associate myself with the views of the New Zealand government expressed in the Emergency Special Session of August, 1958:

First, a political and social revolution of vast scope is taking place in the Middle East as a result of the working of nationalism among the Arab people and their yearning for a better life. It is natural that this revolution should be accompanied by far-reaching changes, that it should have as one of its results a renewal of the sense of kinship among a proud and ancient people and a movement toward a wider measure of unity. It is natural, too, that it should release great constructive energies and that political emancipation should be followed by a desire to free the Arab people from their age-old enemies: poverty and disease.

Secondly, it is, moreover, to be expected that the recently independent Arab countries, in exercising their full freedom to decide their own future, should sometimes differ in adjusting their relations among themselves and with other countries. Such adjustments must naturally bring their own difficulties. But those difficulties clearly ought not to include the development of subversion, indirect aggression, and the systematic and deliberate incitement to violence, as a means of imposing uniformity in the Arab world. There may be one Arab world; but it comprises a number of independent sovereign states. All of these states, as members of the United Nations, are bound under the Charter to practise tolerance and to respect the equal rights of their neighbours. At the Third Emergency Session of August, 1958, they reaffirmed this obligation.

Thirdly, the Soviet Union has played upon existing divisions in the Middle East and has endeavoured to impair long-established and mutually beneficial commercial and political relationships between Middle East countries and the Western democracies, and to make its own influence pre-eminent.

Fourthly, there is the persistence of the Palestine problem which continues to feed Arab hostility to Israel and to threaten international peace and security.

Finally, there is the mounting need for co-operative measures, in which the Western world must share, to develop the Middle East's economic resources and to ensure their employment for the betterment of the people of the area.

There is a further inescapable issue: I refer to the place to be occupied by the Middle East in Great Power relations. It seems hardly necessary to emphasize the responsibility resting on the major powers. The recognition of this undeniable fact does not, of course, mean that other countries outside the region do not have an important part to play. Nor does it carry any implication that the major powers could, or would, attempt any accommodation among themselves which did not have the understanding and approval of the governments which are sovereign in their own Middle Eastern homelands. But, having regard to the influence which the policies of the permanent members of the Security Council must inevitably exert on the future of the Middle East, the New Zealand government regretted that in 1958, it was not found possible to arrange a meeting of heads of government within the framework of the Security Council. It had been our hope that a meeting at this level within the United Nations setting would have encouraged frank exchanges among smaller groups of the countries concerned. It would have permitted the consideration of proposals designed to safeguard the Middle East against domestic turmoil and external threat. And it would, in particular, have enabled the top-level participants to explore agreement on restraint of arms to Middle Eastern countries, on frontier guarantees, and on some measure of neutralisation of the area.

In our concern over Berlin we neglect at our peril the solution of the long-standing problems of the Middle East.

CHAPTER XIII

An Army of Peace

There is no alternative to peace.

—President Eisenhower

A war can no longer be regarded as an extension of policy by other means, when the chapter which it opens may be so apocalyptic as to be a negation of policy. Now that war has become something which could mean the end of the race or even the end of life itself, the old axioms which regarded war and peace as a not-intolerable alternation are worthless. We need a new set of principles.

—The Honourable George Pearkes, Canadian Minister of Defence on April 3, 1959

IN THE TWENTIETH CENTURY MEN HAVE HAD TWO CONFLICTING aspirations: one for disarmament and the other for an international force to curb and check the lawless. The realisation of the horrors of nuclear war has intensified everywhere the yearning for disarmament. But the realisation, even though shared by the Communist dictators and their peoples, has not prevented aggression since the bomb fell on Hiroshima. The path toward disarmament is strewn with failures, and as long as it remains a distant goal we must stand ready to dissuade a would-be aggressor or to repel him if he launches an attack.

Hence the constant proposals for the creation of an international force to be at the disposal of the United Nations.

These proposals are apt to ignore the deterrents already produced by NATO, SEATO, ANZUS, and to a lesser degree by the Baghdad Pact. I have listened to many debates in the Political Committee where the Russians and their satellites have thundered against these defensive organizations. One expects this. If it had not been for NATO, buttressed by the Marshall Plan, Western Europe probably would have succumbed to communism. SEATO probably has deterred Red China from aggression against Thailand and Southern Vietnam. ANZUS, a defensive alliance between the United States, Australia, and New Zealand, stands guard in the Pacific.

In Soviet eyes it does not matter that regional organizations like NATO, SEATO, and ANZUS are expressly sanctioned by the Charter. Their sin is that they stand in the way of the march of Moscow and Peking. Accordingly, one expects Moscow and Peking to blast the West for daring to defend itself. What is less expected and more disappointing is that a group of neutralist states should be as hostile to NATO and SEATO as the Communists. Such are Yugoslavia, Iraq under its recent government, the United Arab Republic, India, and Indonesia.

I have often heard Krishna Menon denounce the defensive pacts. One of his arguments appears to be that if NATO is involved in war, the states adhering to SEATO and the Baghdad Pact automatically will come into the conflict on the side of NATO. As NATO will use atomic weapons, these will be used also by the forces at the disposal of the SEATO and Baghdad powers. And the whole world, belligerent and neutral alike, so the argument runs, will be consumed in the holocaust of nuclear catastrophe. The weak point in Mr. Menon's argument is that it ignores the fact that the very purpose of the West's defensive regional pacts is to prevent the holocaust which he fears. I am satisfied that a majority in the West believes that so far this purpose has been achieved.

Of course the Indian government objects to the adherence of Pakistan to SEATO and the Baghdad Pact. These organizations are directed against the threat of armed attack on any member and, in the case of SEATO, also against the threat of indirect aggression. Thus the members of the Baghdad Pact have agreed to co-operate for their own security and defence. Surely Pakistan could not invoke the Pact if she launched an attack on India over the Kashmir quarrel. The Pact is not available to help an aggressor. Unfortunately there was never any sound domestic support for the Pact in Iraq, and after the murder of the King and Nuri as-Said, Iraq's defection was certain and the Pact was gravely weakened.

The desire of certain undeveloped countries, whether large or small, to remain neutral and aloof from the profound division between democracies and the Communist states is understandable. They wish for time so as to win prosperity. We should not forget the United States tried to stay neutral until the middle of two world wars. But she found, in the famous phrase of Quentin Reynolds, that "only the stars are neutral" in the opposition of two great and irreconcilable forces.

In any major wars of the future the so-called neutralists are likely to learn the same lesson. I say "so-called" because countries like India and Burma deny that they are neutrals. They simply say that they will not join defensive blocs, which in their judgment eventually lead to wars. They recognise the difference between good and evil and pin their faith on the United Nations.

The question is whether, in their own interests and security and as the United Nations is now constituted and organised, this is enough. The United Nations and India herself have proved powerless to help Tibet, a fact which in New Delhi must have given rise to some uneasy reflections. Even though Tibet was not an independent state qualified for membership in the United Nations, it was entitled to preserve its autonomy within the confines of Communist China. There was no defensive organization in existence and capable of coming to its aid.

What then to do? Should the United Nations have available a permanent police (sometimes called peace) force to check aggression? A permanent force at the disposition of the Security Council or the Assembly would not be a new concept. The Charter, through Chapter VII, expressly provides for such a force at the disposition of the Council. Nevertheless, the force has never come into being because the West and the Soviet Union have never reached agreement of the five Great Powers. There is a military staff committee at United Nations headquarters. They meet every month, but they never reach an agreement.

Under Chapter VII the Security Council would have enjoyed its most extensive powers, whereby it could take such action by air, sea, or land forces as might be necessary to maintain or restore international peace. All members of the United Nations undertook to make available to the Council armed forces, assistance, and facilities. They were required to hold immediately available national air-force contingents for combined international enforcement action. The size and the nature of the forces were to be determined by special agreements between the Security Council and each state.

These provisions of the Charter meant, in effect, that the Council could utilise the armed forces of a state without that state's consent. This power was limited for the benefit of the permanent members of the Security Council, each of which by exercising its right of veto could of course prevent any enforcement action, whether involving the use of its own armed forces or not. Once the Security Council had taken a decision to use force, however, the use of any national component of the international police was not subject to the agreement of the state supplying them. To this extent, the Council would have enjoyed supranational powers. Except for the five Great Powers, therefore, it will be seen that the signatories of the Charter agreed to a very considerable potential limitation of their sovereignty.

In an important speech delivered at Copenhagen on May 2, 1959, Mr. Hammarskjold said:

Chapter VII of the United Nations Charter authorizes, in certain circumstances, the Security Council to use military force to maintain peace. It is important to realize what this means. This is not collective security of a kind which a defensive alliance can provide. The Charter expressly permits the formation of such alliances, but the United Nations itself is something else again. The possibilities of the Organization to use military force are limited to acts of coercion in the name of the world community against a nation which violates the peace. Such an action requires unanimity of the Great Powers. This unanimity has a twofold significance. Without it a military police action lacks the foundation necessary to be fully effective. And without it the United Nations would also, in contrast to the fundamental idea on which it is built, be capable of transformation into an instrument of military force in a conflict between the Great Powers—with all that this might mean for the other member states. The rule of unanimity with the right to form defensive alliances defines the position of the Organization. It has never been meant as an organ of collective security of the alliance type, but it is aimed at a universal system for the maintenance of peace which may have, as a natural complement, defensive alliances.

However one-sidedly the veto may have been abused in practice, the hard fact remains—and I am sure I am right in this—that *none* of the Great Powers even now would be willing to relinquish its right of veto in a case where the use of its own armed forces might be required. The failure to confer on the Security Council the enforcement provisions of the Charter cannot be put down simply to short-sightedness on the part of its authors. Even at San Francisco in 1945 the existence of potentially serious differences among the Great Powers was plain enough. But if unity did not then exist, it still was necessary to presuppose it for the future if any real teeth were to be given to the new organization. The Security Council has never grown its teeth.

It is true that the Security Council in 1958 succeeded in establishing in Lebanon a corps of 500 observers limited largely to officers recruited in a score of countries. The Secretary-General was the delegate of the Council to set up the corps and administer it. Ultimate responsibility for the corps was to the Council itself. The Secretary-General has pointed out that the corps, however useful its military training was, did not have even those military functions accorded to UNEF, and of its three leaders two were civilians.

Now we come to what the Assembly has done and can do. It has one extraordinary achievement to its credit: the establishment of the United Nations Emergency Force in 1956. The Secretary-General issued a report on this Force on October 9, 1958, entitled "Summary Study of the Experience Derived from the Establishment and Operation of UNEF." I earnestly commend my readers to study this report, an invaluable document for those who urge or oppose the establishment of a permanent peace force.

Let me give some of the main conclusions of the report, interspersed with some of my own conclusions:

a. The Force, the creation of the Assembly as a result of the Uniting for Peace procedures, is of an *ad hoc* and temporary character.

b. The Force entered Egypt only with the consent of the Egyptian government and can stay in the Gaza Strip and the area of Sharm el Sheikh only so long as the Egyptian government agrees.

c. But as the United Nations and the Egyptian government have each agreed that they will be guided by good faith in the interpretation of the purposes of the Force, a decision by the Egyptian government to ask the Force to leave would require discussion with the United Nations. [Mr. Hammarskjold puts this in language which I find rather difficult to understand. He says that "an exchange of views would be called for toward harmonizing the positions." Perhaps some obscurity is justified.]

d. The components of the force of nearly 6,000 are from member states. [Originally Brazil, Canada, Colombia, Denmark, Finland, India, Indonesia, Norway, Sweden, and Yugoslavia, but Finland and Indonesia have dropped out.]

e. Accordingly, no Great Power contributed men and no power having a special interest in the area. If Egypt, as the host country, objected to any offer of forces, that offer was not accepted. [In 1956 the New Zealand government made the first public offer of a contribution of men; this offer was never accepted. I well remember how difficult I found it to get an answer concerning New Zealand's offer from the Secretariat. The Egyptian government, not unnaturally, was unwilling to have troops on its territory from a state whose government had supported the British action in Egypt.]

f. The sole purpose of the Force, after the British, French, and Israeli forces withdrew, was to maintain quiet in the areas it entered and particularly to prevent the recurrence of incidents in the Gaza Strip. In this it has succeeded. UNEF is not to be used to enforce any specific political solution or to influence the political balance decisive to such a solution. [But in my judgment it is very important to remember that ever since the Force has been in the area of Sharm el Sheikh, the Egyptian government has not attempted to reinstate its blockade of the Strait of Tiran, and Israeli ships have sailed freely in and from the port of Eilat on the Gulf of Aqaba. This development is a significant political result of the presence of UNEF.]

g. The Force can fire only on self-defense and can never take the initiative in the use of arms. It is much more than an observer corps but much less than an army having military objectives. The Force helps to maintain order and has power to arrest infiltrators.

h. The Force has an international character as a subsidiary organ of the General Assembly, which appoints its commander. But the commander operates under the instructions and guidance of the Secretary-General, who in turn is responsible to the Assembly. The Secretary-General has an advisory committee of seven representatives of member states [none of them Great Powers] over which he presides and which assist him in the planning and operation of the Force.

i. The Assembly has decided that all members shall pay rateably the costs of the Force, save those expenses which in any case contributing countries would have to meet under their normal domestic policy. Accordingly, the United Nations pays cost of transportation and allowances to troops over and above these costs which the government concerned would have been obliged to pay in any event. [Mr. Hammarskjold gave a cautious approval to the enunciation of the principles governing the establishment of a standby force, but according to my reading of his report he did not advocate clearly the immediate creation of such a force.]

There is no doubt that the principles and practices which I have enumerated from the Secretary-General's report will be useful guides for the future, if any standby force similar to UNEF is established. They have a bearing on the question of the establishment of a United Nations force in Berlin. Mr. Hammarskjold is particularly emphatic that no United Nations force can be established on the territory of a member state without that member's consent and then only so long as such member agrees.

In our present state of international law, with sovereignty little diminished by the Charter and with nationalism so strong, I concede that these principles enunciated by the Secretary-General are valid and recognised. In 1958 the United States justified its landing in Lebanon because the government of Lebanon requested the arrival of American forces. The British secured similar consent for the stationing of their troops in Jordan. On the other hand, the landing of Anglo-French troops in Egypt in 1956 is generally considered illegal because it was done against the will of the Egyptian government. In any case the Assembly may recommend only the establishment of troops on the territory of a member state and has no power to force a member to accept such troops.

Whether a host country, once it has agreed to accept a United Nations force, should have a decisive voice in the nature of its composition probably will remain a matter of dispute. I hope that the Assembly will have the decisive voice, having evaluated the wishes of the host country. These considerations and many others show how difficult will be the establishment of a permanent peace force which in 1958 was urged by President Eisenhower when I presided over the Emergency Assembly. He described his proposal as a matter for urgent and positive action. He was not the first to urge the establishment of such a force.

Lester Pearson, at present leader of the opposition in Canada, in an article in *Foreign Affairs* of April, 1957, wrote cogently:

> The very least each of our governments can now do, it seems to me, is to draft, in accordance with our respective

constitutional processes, whatever measures are required to place us on a better position to support agreed decisions of the United Nations in an emergency. Are we to go on from crisis to crisis improvising in haste? Or can we now pool our experience and our resources, so that the next time we, the governments and peoples whom the United Nations represents, will be ready and prepared to act?

At various times I myself have suggested a permanent police force. I have considered that a small corps should be available at headquarters so as to be ready in an emergency. In addition, a small force of say 20,000 men should be stationed at some strategic point, from which they could be rushed to a danger spot by the Security Council; or if it failed because of the veto, by the Assembly acting under the Uniting for Peace procedure. The United Kingdom supports the proposal for the establishment of a stand-by force.

Like UNEF, this force would be composed of men from the smaller powers, and its finances similarly provided for. The cost would be great, but the insurance premium would be small. Officials in the United Nations Section of the State Department are said to estimate that it would cost about $25 million a year to maintain an international police force of 6,000 men. But as Max Freedman has said, this expenditure would be a trifling amount when set against the cost of a single new bomber. It might be that the United Nations would have to bear a greater proportion of the cost than it does for UNEF, especially as the contributories might be reluctant to keep many of their troops abroad for lengthy periods, even allowing for replacements.

In addition to a permanent force at a strategic point, members should be asked, on the analogy of Chapter VII of the Charter, to undertake to make available to the Assembly armed forces, assistance and facilities to meet an emergency as and when it should arise and as determined by the Assembly. The size and the nature of the forces to be held in readiness would be determined by special agreement between the Assembly and each state.

The responsibility to direct the use of any of the forces I have suggested could not be delegated in general terms to the Secretary-General. In expressing what is indeed the view of the Secretary-General—specific authorisations to him are another matter—I realise the difficulty of securing speed in an emergency involving a threat to the peace, a weakness inherent in the United Nations. This in certain cases can be overcome by interim action by a power at the request of an endangered state, as in the Lebanese and Jordan crises of 1958. Later, the United Nations force could take over from the power which at the request of the state in peril has stepped in to meet the threat. The Assembly would be more likely to act with speed if it had a force immediately available.

I do not minimise the importance of the United Nations Emergency Force, the establishment of which by the Assembly I regard as more momentous in its way than the creation of the United Nations force in Korea, of which it must be remembered that first, it was authorised by the Security Council only because the Russians were absent from the crucial meeting, and, second, only sixteen nations contributed to the force, the bulk of responsibility falling on the United States, which already had forces in the area.

Lester Pearson, in the article in *Foreign Affairs* also said:

The type of Security Council action against aggression in Korea, therefore, is not likely to be repeated. In any event, the United Nations character of that action was as much symbolic as it was real, because the United States supplied most of the forces and exercised most of the control over them. In so far as the possibility of using the United Nations for collective security was concerned, Korea was both an encouragement and a warning.

Invaluable as UNEF has proved, it may not be a precedent for similar action in the future. During the Lebanese crisis there was no enthusiasm either in the Security Council or in the Assembly for the dispatch of anything more than an observer corps to Lebanon. Jordan rejected the idea of even such a corps. Nevertheless, the danger of another emergency has persuaded many responsible leaders of the necessity for a permanent United Nations Force, created by the Assembly and at its disposal, as an indispensable instrument for the preservation of the rule of law.

I do not minimise the difficulties. Neither the Soviet Union nor, among others, India will support the idea—the Soviet because it wishes to preserve the jurisdiction of the Security Council where its veto can prevent effectively any permanent force being created. Outside the Communist bloc, other states have domestic and external problems into which they have no desire to see the United Nations intrude.

If there was difficulty in persuading some members of the Assembly to pass the November, 1957, resolution with its financial obligation on all members to pay for UNEF, the opposition would be even greater if an attempt were made to create a permanent force. Those who would form such a force would include the small powers whose sacrifices would be considerable, even allowing for over-all United Nations expense. Mr. Eisenhower's proposal was not adopted at the Thirteenth Assembly.

At that Session, on November 5, Mr. Hammarskjold read a closely reasoned statement. He said that following the establishment of UNEF, many of the problems which arose in that type of operation had been solved and tested by experience. He concluded that there was neither reason nor excuse for the United Nations to be unprepared to meet any new emergency requiring similar treatment. In these circumstances, he felt that there was no need for the Assembly to take any action for the present.

I agree with the Secretary-General, save that I say, that there may be new emergencies which do not require similar treatment and which may be solved only if there is a permanent United Nations force or if one may be called together speedily. I urge that studies should proceed immediately in the United Nations, and action be taken on this vital question.

The Secretary-General emphasised the need for the consent of the host country, as well as of contributing countries, to any such operation. In his view, a Peace Supervision Force could enter a country only with the consent of the government of that country. Having regard for Mr. Hammarskjold's conclusion, it is pertinent to ask how such a force could enter West Berlin, where complicated legal questions of jurisdiction are involved. Moreover, the Berlin problem is particularly relevant to France, the United Kingdom, the United States, the Soviet Union, and West Germany. But as peace is indivisible, all members of the United Nations, small as well as great, are vitally concerned.

The Secretary-General emphasised that his approach to the question of a United Nations force was guided by the strictest respect for the rules of the Charter. All will accept his emphasis. He went on to say that his approach was entirely pragmatic and did not try to freeze a pattern of action; nor would it give rise to arrangements conducive to inappropriate use in the future. He emphasised that the political issues had to ✓ be solved.

During the Thirteenth Assembly nothing further was done toward the creation of a permanent peace force, and the item entitled "Summary Study of the Experience Derived from the Establishment and Operation of UNEF" was disposed of. This seems to me a rather summary way of dealing with a summary study following the Secretary-General's valuable statement to the Special Political Committee.

Political issues come and go. Today they have an awkward habit of staying with us for a long time. Concerning Berlin, they have arisen in drastic form. In spite of the primary interest of the Great Powers for the future of Berlin, as the instrument for preserving world peace the United Nations is involved and must be ready to undertake its responsibilities.

I believe, as I have said publicly, that we must persist in attempting to create a permanent force. We must avail ourselves and learn from the improvisations of the Korean, Suez, and Lebanon crises. I agree with Mr. Pearson that member governments, excluding the permanent members of the Security Council, should be invited to signify a willingness in principle to contribute contingents to the United Nations for purposes that are essentially noncombatant, such as, for example, the supervision of agreed cease-fires and comparable peace-supervisory functions.

Yet I believe we may have to go much further than this, perhaps soon. We live on a powder keg. The Berlin crisis is upon us. It may be that the United Nations will have to take part in the solution of that crisis if it is not to burst into ruinous war. A United Nations force in West Berlin, comprised of men from smaller countries, fully armed and capable of fighting a defensive action and with the mission of preserving West Berlin as a democratic outpost, may be one solution. Of course such a force would require adequate and uninterrupted passage from and to the West. If Mr. Khrushchev is in earnest, he should agree to a comparable force in East Berlin, so that the whole city could be under United Nations protection, its freedom ensured. So the present occupying forces could be withdrawn and some degree of disengagement effected.

Alternately the forces of the four Great Powers could remain in Berlin with United Nations forces stationed at points of ingress to and egress from Berlin. Consideration should be given to the establishment of a United Nations presence in Berlin, whereby officials from the world organization could watch the situation there and report to the Secretary-General on any developments threatening or tending to threaten the peace.

Of course there will be difficulties, not the least of which will be securing Soviet consent, which might be granted only if a satellite's troops form part of the force. The Soviet may insist that no NATO countries should contribute to a United Nations force in or around Berlin. This would eliminate a Canadian contribution. But this is no insuperable difficulty to the creation of the force, and I believe that the attempt should be made. The prestige and the usefulness of the United Nations are bound up with its determination to solve the problem of a permanent force. If some of its members, for domestic reasons, continue to oppose the establishment of the force they are threatening the foundation of the United Nations.

In a speech in the Canadian House of Commons on April 3, 1959, the Minister of Defence, George Pearkes, offered a number of points as a basis for discussion, the purpose of which was to focus attention on methods by which the United Nations might provide a framework for any four-power agreement on Berlin. These points were:

> First: The basic role of the UN might be to verify that all parties were abiding by the terms of the agreement.
> Second: An essential part of the agreement would be a Soviet pledge binding itself and its associates to permit full freedom of access to West Berlin and the acceptance of a UN presence on the lines of communications.
> Third: It should be understood that any UN responsibility for West Berlin would be complementary to the present rights and obligations of the four occupying powers.

I am sorry that in his Copenhagen speech Mr. Hammarskjold said that in his view "practical considerations alone prevent even the kind of quasi-military arrangements which are possible under Chapter VII and which fall within the competence of the General Assembly, from being used except to a very limited extent, if at all." Later, the Secretary-General asked whether "the United Nations at present is so organized constitutionally, that there is any organ which would be entrusted with that kind of policy decision back of a potentially fighting force."

I cannot follow this line of reasoning. The United Nations

was behind the fighting force which successfully threw back the Northern Koreans and the Chinese. There were different constitutional questions involved in the establishment of UNEF but they were surmounted, thanks to the pertinacity of the Assembly and the skill of the Secretary-General. I firmly believe that if the powers have the will, the problems of establishing a United Nations force capable of fighting a delaying action to protect Berlin could be solved.

CHAPTER XIV

A Step Toward Harmony in Outer Space

Man presumes much when he presumes to bring the dominion of the stars within the purview of his legislative processes and under the jurisdiction of his administrative agencies.

Space is infinite. Man's knowledge of space is finite. The sum of our understanding is not yet sufficient for us to comprehend how vast are the dimensions of our ignorance. We delude ourselves—at considerable peril —when, with small fragments of fact and fancy, we attempt to construct an image of the future after the pattern of our own past experience. We have no frame of reference by which to visualize the design of tomorrow.

We may, as some say, stand now at the edge of the battleground for Armageddon. Or we may, as others believe, be poised before the plains of the millennium. In either event, we have no national option but to marshal our resources, order our course, and proceed beyond the shelter and sanctuary of Earth's atmosphere into this realm of the limitless unknown.

To proceed prudently, or to proceed at all, we must of necessity proceed by faith. Humility is a proper traveling companion for this national journey.

From the Introduction to the Report by Senator Lyndon Johnson of Texas, from the Special Committee on Space and Astronautics. June 11, 1958.

I SHALL NEVER FORGET THE IMPACT ON THE TWELFTH ASSEMBLY of the announcement that a Soviet sputnik had reached outer space. Among the undeveloped nations the prestige of the Soviet grew over night. But it was speedily seen that although the ascent of the sputnik was the amazing achievement of one nation, the consequences would affect all mankind, whether for good or evil. Man's horizons would no longer be of this earth. Eventually he may succeed in reaching the moon and the stars and penetrating the mysteries of the universe. If he travels so far for peaceful purposes, the consequences and gains for his future beggar description. If he uses outer space for purposes of war, probably he will reduce the world to a shambles.

Fortunately, as a primary condition of man's existence there is world-wide recognition of the need for ordered relationships in the use of outer space. Unfortunately, the approach to the subject is plagued by the seemingly irreconcilable and certainly profound division between the Communist and the non-Communist worlds. Each recognises the need for the peaceful use of outer space, but at the height of the discussions in the Thirteenth Assembly of the United Nations, the Soviet said that it would boycott the Assembly's Ad Hoc Committee, established to study the problems of outer space. The boycott continues. Yet the world should not abandon hope. It can take heart from the fact that in the Thirteenth Assembly the question found its way onto the agenda, a useful resolution was passed and the Committee, although without Soviet participation, has commenced important studies.

As President of the Twelfth Assembly, I had urged that it should, as a matter of urgency, deal with the problems of the peaceful use of outer space—if necessary in a special session. On November 22, 1957, I said to the New Jersey State Bar Association:

> As to the actual convening of states on problems raised by recent and imminent ventures into outer space, I believe that the United Nations is the proper forum for necessary discussion. First of all, it is peculiarly equipped to provide small powers with an opportunity to be heard. Although it is undeniable that primary responsibility for the settlement of such matters rests on the Great Powers, any steps taken by them would necessarily affect the smaller ones and I therefore believe, both personally and as a representative of a small power, that they definitely should be heard. Public opinion throughout the world must not be overlooked, and citizens of a small country must be given an equal chance as citizens of a big country to make their feelings known on such important matters.
>
> Choice of the United Nations as the forum for the consideration of problems relating to outer space is also supported by the identity between its purposes and principles which must govern any international consideration of such problems. If one or more nations have achieved something which can take us into outer space, the peaceful use of such a device must be assured, and this through some program of international control. Further, the benefits derived from such devices must be shared by all nations, in keeping with the growing tendency of international sharing of advances in the scientific field, a tendency which has been accentuated in the field of atomic energy and in the arrangements adopted for the International Geophysical Year.

Other voices around the world were soon heard in support of this general approach; all emphasised the urgency of the matter. The President of the United States, in his message of January 12, 1958, to Mr. Bulganin, proposed that the United

States and the Soviet Union should agree that outer space should be used only for peaceful purposes. Mr. Eisenhower said forcefully that we face a decisive moment in history. Following this message the late John Foster Dulles suggested an international commission, preferably under the auspices of the United Nations, which would be comparable to the International Atomic Energy Agency. The latter sees that nuclear materials which it disposes of are used for peaceful purposes.

On March 15, 1958, the Soviet permanent representative to the United Nations asked that an item banning the use of cosmic space for military purposes be included on the provisional agenda of the Thirteenth Assembly. However, this Soviet proposal was linked to a demand for the elimination of foreign bases. Nevertheless, the Soviet's accompanying memorandum for the purposes of international co-operation in the study of cosmic space deserves serious study.

On May 19, 1958, Dag Hammarskjold made a useful contribution when he expressed the hope "that the General Assembly, as a result of its consideration, would find the way to an agreement on a basic rule that outer space, and the celestial bodies therein, are not considered as capable of appropriation by any state, and that it would further affirm the overriding interest of the community of nations in the peaceful and beneficial use of outer space and 'initiate' steps for an international machinery to further this end. Were the General Assembly to reach this point, the governments co-operating in the United Nations would have laid what seems to me to be a valid basis for the future development, in international cooperation, of the use of outer space for the benefit of all."

Mr. Hammarskjold's view that celestial bodies should not be considered capable of appropriation by any state is strengthened by the fact that no government has questioned the right of either the Soviet Union or the United States to send satellites through outer space. No government has claimed that its sovereignty is infringed when a satellite hurtles through outer space far above its territory. The Soviet Union, which claims to have hurled a rocket to the moon, does not make any claim to sovereignty over the moon.

It is significant that on September 18, 1958, in his policy speech in the general debate of the Thirteenth Assembly, Mr. Dulles chose this forum to expound his views on man's major strides in his "conquest of his newest and most exciting frontier, outer space." Mr. Dulles asserted that in establishing a system of control of outer space we cannot await a comprehensive disarmament program. I agree that we should not await such a program, but as intermediate range and intercontinental ballistic missiles would traverse outer space, its peaceful use is linked with disarmament and with the basic problem of a world divided by two conflicting ideologies.

Mr. Dulles, well aware of these manifold difficulties, nevertheless cogently said:

> Ten precious years were lost in the development of the peaceful uses of nuclear energy because full international cooperation was not promptly begun. We cannot afford a similar delay in this vast new dimension of human experience which offers perhaps an even greater challenge and opportunity than the splitting of the atom.

The Secretary of State proposed to the Assembly that it establish a representative Ad Hoc Committee to report to the next Assembly on: the activities and resources of the United Nations and its specialized agencies relating to outer space; the nature of specific projects of international co-operation in outer space which could not be undertaken under United Nations auspices; and useful United Nations' organizational arrangements to facilitate international co-operation in this field.

Mr. Dulles hoped that these proposals would receive unanimous support. He was doomed to disappointment. His hopes were wrecked on the rocks of Communist opposition and intransigence. It is true that the Assembly on December 13, 1958, established an eighteen-nation Ad Hoc Committee for the purposes outlined by Mr. Dulles. But there were not enough Communist countries on the Committee to satisfy the Soviet Union. Accordingly, the nine-member Communist bloc voted against the resolution, serving notice that they would not participate. In the absence of the Soviet Union, with its knowledge and success in outer space, the Committee will find difficulty in functioning with full effectiveness. This Soviet boycott is lamentable.

Aside from the nature of outer space, undoubtedly questions will arise as to sovereignty over celestial bodies which man may reach in the foreseeable future. We must consider whether these celestial bodies should be regarded as subject to claims of sovereignty and, if so, whether the rules of international law regarding discovery and occupation, conquest, and cession should be made applicable. Space ships presumably would need to be subjected to some legal order, and this raises the question of the applicability of present laws, both national and international, regarding aircraft and seagoing vessels.

My own view is that international law, as we know it, giving title by occupation, possession, and settlement, is not applicable to celestial bodies. We should consider the non-military and the military aspects of the problem.

The nonmilitary aspects are concerned with the so-called satellites and the means of delivering them. International agreements concerning the satellites which now orbit and in the future will orbit the globe, including the means of launching them, should be made. The launching of satellites does not appear to impinge on the disarmament problem, and the data about them is to be exchanged through the project known as the International Geophysical Year. I believe that any nation about to launch a satellite should register with the United Nations notice of its intention to do so, giving particulars as to the nature of the orbit. Scientists are aware that there is the prospect of satellites being used for reconnaissance—for taking photographs of places on the world. This could be a military use and is not to be ignored. Having made this observation, I come to the military aspects of the problem.

We are concerned with the means of delivering missiles into outer space. Because missiles were developed primarily for military purposes, their connection with disarmament is obvious. We are all aware of intercontinental ballistic missiles: ICBM; and intermediate range ballistic missiles: IRBM.

It is obvious why the Soviet Union has linked the banning of the use of cosmic space for military purposes to a proposal for "the elimination of foreign military bases on the territories of other states, primarily in Europe, the Near and Middle East and North Africa." It is from such bases that the NATO powers could launch IRBM's. If the Soviet were to secure the prohibition of this, it would gain for itself a lopsided advantage.

We know that agreement among the three nuclear powers on the control of outer space, with respect to the problems of disarmament, will be extremely difficult. Even though at the present time the differences among the powers may seem almost insuperable, the interested countries should reach some agreement on a technical and scientific basis.

Before reaching an effective agreement on the control of the various missiles designed to take objects into outer space, one could envisage proposals that inspectors should be fully informed of such matters as: the location of launching sites; details of construction including the size of missiles, the nature of the materials used, propellant fuels, etc.; and the specific purposes for which satellites are being launched. The latter would presumably necessitate the inspection of each satellite on its launching site.

The availability of knowledge on these points, which would be necessary for effective control, shows how far-reaching such an agreement would be. Clearly, the pervasive nature of the information which would have to be exchanged might be regarded as the last and most advanced stage of agreement on disarmament. In the present state of distrust, many decisions must be made effective before this last stage can be reached. The race to develop the ICBM, considered by many to be the ultimate weapon in nuclear warfare, involves the most sensitive areas of national security.

At least the principle has been established that the control of outer space is one for the Assembly of the United Nations to consider: an Assembly where great and small powers alike present their views and proposals on matters affecting the present and future of all mankind. The Soviet Union itself recognised the wisdom of establishing the jurisdiction of the Assembly in its proposals of March 15, 1958, perverted even as these were by their reference to overseas bases. The majority of the members of the United Nations have shown their anxiety to utilise outer space, under the aegis of the United Nations, for the benefit and not for the destruction of mankind.

The Ad Hoc Committee probably will confront two different approaches: first by those who now and quickly would draft conventions settling questions of sovereignty in outer space and deciding, we shall say, that no state in the future can claim sovereignty to the moon, or any part of it, simply because of a first landing on and occupation of part of the moon.

On the other hand, the Committee will hear those arguing against the immediate preparation of a detailed and logical convention dealing with the sovereignty and the use of outer space. In the words of Loftus Becker, legal adviser to the State Department, sensible solutions cannot now be evolved to future problems whose nature and content cannot be accurately foreseen. The exponents of this view are likely to be influenced by some of the difficulties confronted on the question of the definition of territorial waters in the recent conference on the Law of the Sea.

I am not unduly disturbed by these two different approaches. I believe that a middle way will be found, that some general principles will be enunciated, and that an international agency for the use of outer space for peaceful purposes eventually will be established. The great point is that the subject has come within the purview of the world organization, where it properly belongs, as the repository of the hopes and the aspirations of mankind.

CHAPTER XV

The Challenge of Tomorrow

THE FATEFUL QUESTION FOR THE FUTURE OF THE UNITED
Nations is whether it will prove an effective forum for the
settlement of great political problems. The democracies failed
to use the League to check Japan in Manchuria and to save
Abyssinia from Mussolini. Of course the League continued its
work in secondary activities, but its members had stultified
it in its primary purpose to curb an aggressor. The League
foundered on the rocks of aggression in Manchuria and Abyssinia.

The architects of the United Nations, remembering the
melancholy lessons learnt by the League, sought to give teeth
to the Security Council; but it has never grown the teeth its
hopeful parents expected. In the one great crisis that the
Council handled effectively it borrowed the teeth of the
United States and a few other members. Southern Korea was
saved. But in the future the Soviet will not permit the Council
to use such effective dentists.

No amount of sentimental optimism and wishful thinking
can ever blind us to the consequences of the questions posed
by C. Wilfred Jenks, in his scholarly book *The Common Law
of Mankind:*

What, however, is the value of renouncing war, of providing facilities for the judicial development of the law, of improving the international legislative process and promoting an ever widening network of obligations under multipartite instruments, and of looking to international organizations to make an important contribution to the more vigorous development of customary law, unless there is a minimum of assurance that respect for law and order will be maintained and when necessary, enforced? Without an effective secular arm at its disposal, international law has more in common with the theology than government.

To that conclusion the people of Hungary are likely to say a melancholy amen. It does not help to console ourselves, by pointing to all the useful work done by the United Nations and its subsidiary organs in the fields of health, labor, economics, communications, and so forth. Of course this work is important and plays its part in promoting conditions necessary for the preservation of peace. But such subsidiary organs could exist apart from the United Nations. The acid test will be whether the members of the United Nations, in it and through it, will be able to stop an aggressor in a case similar to that of Hungary.

If Hungary is excluded, the record certainly justifies the existence and the continuance of the United Nations. To take only one area: without the intervention of the world organization in the Middle East following the outbreak of hostilities between the Arab states and Israel, no armistice would have been achieved. Because of the continued participation in the affairs of the Middle East by the Security Council, the Assembly, the Secretariat and its staff in the field, war has not been resumed save for the conflict of 1956. The Assembly intervened successfully in the Suez crisis and later in 1958 in the Lebanese and Jordan crises.

But still the nagging questions arise: Has enough been done and is the machinery of the United Nations likely to cope effectively in the Middle East with emergencies like Suez? The second question must be asked because the awkward fact is that the members of the United Nations, great and small, have not come to grips with the substance of Middle Eastern problems. As long as they fail to do so, the United Nations is sitting on a volcano. It is true that the chief responsibility for settling Middle Eastern questions lies with the parties themselves. Nevertheless, they need the help of all members. Unfortunately, most members of the United Nations deal with the effects in the area and not with the remedy of the causes.

One of the principal causes of unrest and conflict along the borders of Israel is the presence of nearly a million refugees whose plight grows as their numbers increase. But year after year in one of the main committees in which Israel and the Arab states air their grievances we are treated to a futile debate following which a few states, led by the United States and Britain, continue to contribute to the bare maintenance of the refugees. But no headway is made toward the solution of the vital problem of the permanent resettlement and rehabilitation of these unfortunate people.

So long as this melancholy situation continues, the Middle East is likely to erupt. Whether we relish it or not, the Soviet Union is a power to be reckoned with from the Caspian to the Persian Gulf and the Red Sea. Moscow uses misery and unrest in the area to spread communism and to extend Russian influence and power in Arab countries, as Colonel Nasser has learnt. The oil of Iraq and Iran is an irresistible lure to the Kremlin. For some years now I have observed the representatives of the Soviet Union voting as the Arab states desire. I hope that this practice is coming to an end, for communism and the Muslim way of life should have nothing in common.

The point remains: in a strategic section afflicted with poverty and instability, although with vast resources of oil, where the causes of present and potential trouble are not being removed, will the United Nations through its members prove itself capable of dealing with the inevitable explosion? Problems of this magnitude may be dealt with outside the United Nations through meetings at the summit. I would be sorry if the United Nations, with all its facilities for diplomacy, were to be thus bypassed. This would have an inevitable effect on its prestige. As the Secretary-General has said, the United Nations is in effect an instrument of diplomacy for and among nations.

The general public has had the dubious advantage of watching on television the great debates of the Security Council, the Assembly, and its committees. I say "dubious" because while the people have learnt something of United Nations personalities and procedures and of member governments, diplomacy by television is not the best way of allaying tensions and cooling national passions.

What is overlooked is that in the great building beside the East River quiet diplomacy proceeds behind the scenes, especially during an Assembly session. The Security Council may meet whenever it so decides; its members, which of course include the Great Powers, may confer in private. I have often wished that the rule whereby foreign ministers and members may take their seats automatically were invoked more often, and that foreign ministers gathered more often in the United Nations and, if the Press will forgive me, frequently in closed session. With the Secretary-General playing his unique part, the United Nations could then be used to better advantage.

Unfortunately, Mr. Khrushchev does not seem to show any marked enthusiasm for the United Nations or, for that matter, for foreign ministers, whom he regards as superfluities. The result is that we must have meetings at the summit, for only in this way, so it is said, can Mr. Khrushchev be reached. The first meeting at the summit was far from a success and was characterized by that imprecision which ill-prepared meetings, even of the great, are likely to reveal, particularly when there has been no real meeting of minds and the parties have objectives and ways of thought that differ widely.

I am far from claiming that the United Nations is the only forum where international disputes can be settled. The Charter itself hallows the use of diplomacy. The problem of Cyprus appears to have been settled between the United Kingdom, Greece, and Turkey outside the halls of the world organization. Yet I believe that the long debates on this vexed question in the Assembly played their part in leading to this settlement.

In the United Nations there is the machinery for peace through the Security Council, and if it fails, through the Assembly by the use of the Uniting for Peace procedure. That procedure was used successfully in the Suez crises, but not in the Hungarian tragedy. One failure has not nullified the procedure. That failure only serves to emphasise the overwhelming need to use the procedure successfully in the future. The United Nations must gain a secular arm. The organization has such an arm in the Gaza strife. Surely this example will inspire all its members to create a permanent peace force to deter and curb a future aggressor.

In an imperfect world riven by the division between the democracies and the Communists the United Nations is and will continue to be the chief agency for reconciliation and pacification. Only within the Assembly do almost all the nations of the world sit in conference and debate, watched by mankind and urged by millions of lonely voices to save them from catastrophe. The United Nations cannot fail, for its dissolution would be the knell of all men's hopes and plans and prayers for peace and survival.

If I am right it will be a slow business for our people to reach rational views, assuming that we are allowed to work peaceably to that end. But as I grow older I grow calm. If I feel what are perhaps an old man's apprehensions, that competition from new races will cut deeper than working men's disputes and will test whether we can hang together and can fight; if I fear that we are running through the world's resources at a pace that we cannot keep; I do not lose my hopes. I do not pin my dreams for the future to my country or even to my race. I think it probable that civilization somehow will last as long as I care to look ahead—perhaps with smaller numbers, but perhaps also bred to greatness and splendor by science. I think it not improbable that man, like the grub that prepares a chamber for the winged thing it never has seen but is to be—that man may have cosmic destinies that he does not understand. And so beyond the vision of battling races and an impoverished earth I catch a dreaming glimpse of peace.

The other day my dream was pictured to my mind. It was evening. I was walking homeward on Pennsylvania Avenue near the Treasury, and as I looked beyond Sherman's Statue to the west the sky was aflame with scarlet and crimson from the setting sun. But, like the note of downfall in Wagner's opera, below the sky line there came from little globes the pallid discord of the electric lights. And I thought to myself the Götterdämmerung will end, and from those globes clustered like evil eggs will come the new masters of the sky. It is like the time in which we live. But then I remembered the faith that I partly have expressed, faith in a universe not measured by our fears, a universe that has thought and more than thought inside of it, and as I gazed, after the sunset and above the electric lights there shone the stars.

Justice Oliver Wendell Holmes

INDEX

Index

179